QUILLING
Desert flowers

Jean Woolston-Hamey

Kangaroo Press

This book is dedicated to my good friend Viv Grace. Her encouragement and assistance has been very much appreciated.

QUILLING DESERT FLOWERS
First published in Australia in 2003 by Kangaroo Press
an imprint of Simon & Schuster (Australia) Pty Ltd,
20 Barcoo Street, East Roseville NSW 2069

A Viacom Company
Sydney New York London

Visit our website at www.simonsaysaustralia.com

The National Library of Australia
Cataloguing-in-Publication data

   Woolston-Hamey, Jean.
      Quilling : desert flowers

      ISBN 0 7318 1178 X.

      Paper quillwork. I. Title.

745.54

Cover and internal design Anna Warren, Warren Ventures Pty Ltd
Typeset in 12/16pt Bembo
Printed in China through Colorcraft Ltd., Hong Kong

Photography: Bob Weeks, Coffs Harbour NSW
Illustrations: Anna Warren, Warren Ventures Pty Ltd

10 9 8 7 6 5 4 3 2 1

CONTENTS

INTRODUCTION

This book came to life after a visit from a friend living in Western Australia. As part of her work in managing the Comet Gold Mine she needed to find unique gift cards depicting the local flora. It is an awesome experience seeing the vast expanses of wildflowers that fill the deserts after summer rains.

In this collection of desert flowers, I have tried to include some of the less well known native flowers. Most people are familiar with the Sturt's Desert Pea but not the Native Orange, which is a bush tucker food. The Jarrah is thought of as a large tree but it also grows in a smaller form as a multi-stem shrub-like plant. So I have taken this opportunity to explore some of the other wonderful flowers that inhabit the diverse desert areas of inland Australia. Places like Marble Bar in Western Australia to Uluru in Northern Territory and the Sturt Desert in outback New South Wales, Queensland and South Australia are so unique and alive.

Each time I start a new book I am amazed at how extraordinary our flora is. I am quite sure I am not alone in my passion for Australia's plants and hope that many people find great enjoyment in creating these projects.

I would love to hear from fellow quillers with thoughts of my earlier books or for patterns they would like to see in my future books. My address is PO Box 76 Coffs Harbour, New South Wales, 2450. As my husband Ian and I run a tourist attraction seven days a week, an extra visitor interested in quilling would be made most welcome. Ask any local where Carobana is and the reply will be 'The chocolate factory, oh, that's at Korora just north of town, past the Big Banana'.

MATERIALS AND EQUIPMENT

Each full size pattern is set on 21 cm x 25 cm (8" x 10") card background, this makes them easier to frame.

I have tried to keep the paper sizes to the standard pre-cut widths. You can go a little higher or lower if you get stuck for the exact size.

Two types of paper have been used, 80 gsm photocopy paper and Canson art paper which is usually the paper used in good quality pre-cut papers.

Quilling Tools

Here I have used two types of quilling tools:

1. A slotted tool: a fine metal tube with either a wood or metal handle. This gives a round central hole.
2. A needle tool: a sewing needle with the tip of the eye opened to form a prong; the point of the needle attaches into a wooden handle.

Paper Punches

These can be used for petal shapes.

Other Tools

White PVA glue or craft glue

Small sharp scissors

Fine pen for tracing patterns

Stitch ripper for embossing leaves, the handle of this tool can be used to create concaving

Soft eraser or firm foam pad to concave onto

Craft knife

Measuring ruler

Dimensional paint (colours indicated in instructions)

Small paintbrush to coat inside some quilled pieces and for applying dimensional paint

A fine knitting needle or straight wire for rolling stems

Fine-tip tweezers

BASIC INSTRUCTIONS

In this book I have listened to my fellow quillers and included smaller patterns for small cards and tags. Although the patterns I create look big, they can be made in part for applying to smaller items. The backgrounds of the pieces in this book are only 20 cm x 26.5 cm (8" x 10"). The same sizes were used in my first book. All future books will contain miniature versions of all patterns.

A tight coil is the main quilling shape used as well as large and small cups, cones and bells. Some will take a little patience and a steady hand to make. If you have trouble with unrolling, glue as you go or at regular intervals.

Some fringing can be done with a fringing tool but I prefer to use sharp scissors.

Each main piece is accompanied by a stem chart, which will help you to achieve a natural look to the layout.

Noting the way leaves are attached to the stem is important for a realistic look. Some leaves grow opposite one another on the stem, others are alternate and some are quite irregular.

Some of the small leaf patterns for the main pieces can be used with the gift tags.

If you are mounting the main pieces onto a surface other than cardboard (glass, plastic etc), you will need a stronger mounting glue.

With the little gift tags, you can follow the photograph for the placement of the blossom, bud, leaf, stem and pod or create your own arrangement.

I do hope you find enjoyment in creating this new range of blossoms. Remember, quilling should be enjoyable so don't work at it too hard, just let it flow.

KANGAROO APPLE

Solanum sturtiana

A rather stiff shrub with delicate mauve crumbled flowers. Spring and summer see these flowers appear in large clusters in the drier sandy places of Australia. The soft grey green leaves and stems are typical of dry climate plants. A number of varieties exist and all are related to the humble potato, so some can be eaten as bush tucker. Some have lots of thorns while others only a few. Some can be cultivated for home gardens (in drier areas).

Materials

Canson papers
    Mauve (petals and buds)
    White (blossom centres)
    Yellow (stamen)
    Light grey (stems, leaves and thorns)
    Pale green (stems, leaves, bud cups
    and calyx)
    Hemp (berries)
Scissors
Mauve iridescent dimensional paint to match
    petals
3 mm hole punch (optional)
Embossing tool for mid rib marking
Round ended tool to press petal shaping (I use
    the handle of a stitch ripper)

Construction (needle tool)

Blossoms

Cut 5 petal rounds in mauve, from pattern 1.
Cut 5 petal rounds in mauve, from pattern 2.
Punch or cut a 3 mm hole in the centre of each petal piece.

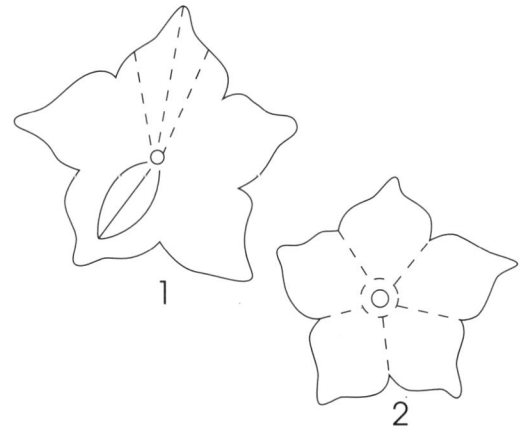

Press – – – areas with round ended tool to shape all petals.

Using dimensional paint mark the elliptical shape as shown on all lobes of petal piece.

Centres for each blossom

FOR LARGER BLOSSOMS
Cut 5 yellow strips 2 mm x 2 cm.
Cut 5 white strips 2 mm x 1 cm.
Join at right angles. See pattern 3.

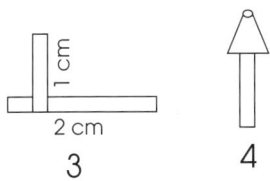

3   4

FOR SMALLER BLOSSOMS

Cut 5 yellow strips 2 mm x 1.5 cm.

Cut 5 white strips 2 mm x 1 cm.

Join as for larger blossom. Both sizes are made the same way.

Coil a cone from free end of yellow strip. Glue so the joining end of the white strip is hidden by the overlapping of the yellow strip. See pattern 4.

Cut 1 white strip 2 mm x 3 cm for each blossom.

Attach 5 stamens in a tight row starting 3 mm from one end. See pattern 5.

Coil from 3 mm end around the middle of the 1 cm strips.

Take petal piece and glue the inside edge of the punched hole. Fit the stamen bundle into the hole so there are equal amounts of the 3 cm white strip above the hole as below. Gentle easement is required for a neat fit.

Calyx (Make 4)

1 for each blossom mounted side on (as desired).

1 pale green strip 2 mm x 7 cm. Coil to long cone. Fit to underside of petal piece to cover the protruding stamen ends. Slightly trim the stamen base ends if necessary for a snug fit.

Buds (Make 3)

Cut 3 mauve strips 3 mm x 18 cm. Coil to a rounded end tall cup. See pattern 6.

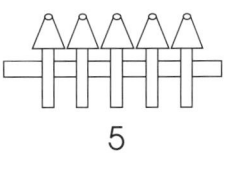

5

6   7

Cut 3 light green strips 3 mm x 18 cm. Coil to a pointed cup. See pattern 7.

Glue open ends together in pairs, 1 mauve with 1 pale green.

Berries (Make 7)

Cut 7 strips hemp 2 mm x 30 cm. Coil to half ball. Coat the inside with glue and allow to dry.

Leaves

Cut 1 light grey rectangle 5 cm x 12 cm.

Cut 1 pale green rectangle 5 cm x 12 cm.

Glue together, apply slight pressure and allow to dry.

Cut 13 leaves from pattern 8.

8

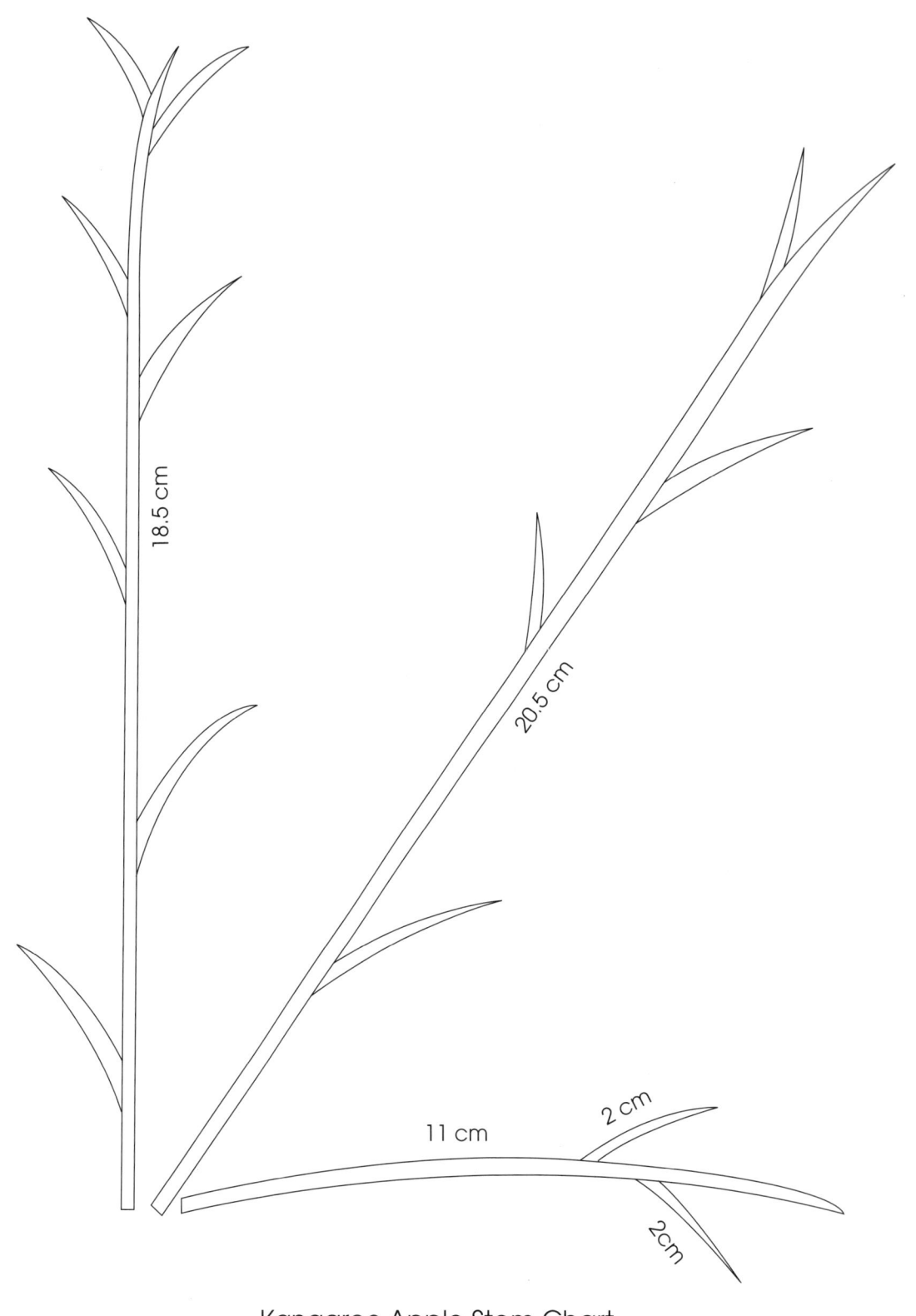

18.5 cm

20.5 cm

11 cm

2 cm

2cm

Kangaroo Apple Stem Chart

Emboss mid rib on pale green side. When mounting, twist some leaves to show grey underside.

Stems

All these are layered on both sides. They are all even at ONE END ONLY.

MAIN STEMS

All 3 mm, 2 are 9 layers, 1 is 5 layers.

1 centre grey 20.5 cm / 2 green 18 cm / 2 grey 16 cm / 2 green 14 cm / 2 grey 12 cm.

1 centre grey 18.5 cm / 2 green 16 cm / 2 grey 14 cm / 2 green 12 cm / 2 grey 10 cm.

1 centre grey 11 cm / 2 green 9 cm / 2 grey 7 cm.

SECONDARY STEMS

All 2 mm, 5 layers

1 centre grey 4cm / 2 green 3 cm / 2 grey 2 cm.

6 centre grey 3 cm / 2 green 2.5 cm / 2 grey 2 cm.

4 centre grey 2 cm / 2 green 1.5 cm / 2 grey 1 cm.

BERRY STEMS

Cut 2 pale green strips 2 mm x 2 cm.

Thorns

7 in light grey 2 mm x 1 cm cut to a fine taper and curve.

Mounting

Attach stems according to chart.

Add blossoms, you can decide how many are side on, so make calyx for each one or just follow the photo. Add buds at top of stems. Add leaves, remember to twist some and curve others. Add berries as pictured. Thorns can vary in number and position, as desired.

Kangaroo Apple — Miniature

(for gift tag 8 cm x 3.5 cm)

Materials

Canson papers

  Mauve (petals, buds)

  White (blossom centres)

  Yellow (stamen)

  Light grey (stems, leaves, thorns)

  Pale green (stems, leaves, bud cups, calyx)

  Hemp (berries)

Mauve dimensional paint

3 mm hole punch (optional)

Embossing tool for mid ribs

Pressing tool (rounded end)

Construction (Make 3)

For each blossom the construction is the same as for the full size piece, only measurements are different.

Cut 3 mauve petal rounds from pattern 9.

Punch or cut the central hole, press on top and underside as shown and add dimensional paint on elliptical shape.

'O' indicates the press points to shape petal. See pattern 10.

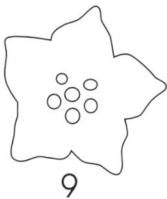

9

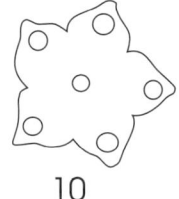

10

Centre

Cut 5 yellow strips 1.5 mm x 1 cm.

Cut 5 white strips 1.5mm x 1cm.

Do not coil a cone but make a straight tight coil.

Cut 1 white strip 2 mm x 3 cm.

Attach stamen to 3 cm white strip and coil. Glue into petal piece and trim protruding ends of stamen on the underside. This will allow the blossom to sit closer to the card.

Leaves

If you have some scraps from the full sized piece, use them or glue a new piece. See pattern 11.

Stems

Cut pale green stems 1.5 mm x 1 cm.

Buds

Cut 1 mauve strip 1.5 mm x 10 cm. See pattern 12.

Cut 1 pale green strip 1.5 mm x 10 cm. See pattern 13.

Join open ends of each together.

Berries

Cut 1 hemp strip 1.5 mm x 15 cm, in a half ball shape.

Position as pictured on gift tags or as desired.

JARRAH
Eucalyptus marginata

Jarrah is a well-known eucalyptus tree from Western Australia. Its growth varies enormously from a large straight tree to a multi-stemmed shrub. Soil type and rainfall strongly influence its shape. Its distinctive leaves are dark glossy green on top with light green underneath. Red brown bark contrasts well against the cream flowers which appear in spring and summer. An Australian film called *The Winds of Jarrah* was made about a timber working family in Western Australia. Parts of the film were filmed not far from Coffs Harbour (where I live) on the Dorrigo Plateau. The Plateau has a very strong timber cutting history and still boasts a mill or two, even now.

Materials

Canson papers
  Pale yellow (blossom fringing)
  Dark green (blossom centres and leaf upper surface)
  Red earth (buds)
  Mid green (bud cups and under leaf)
  Red brown (seed pods and stems)
PVA glue
Scissors
Embossing tool

Construction
(needle and slotted tool)

Blossoms (Make 30)
Cut 30 cream strips 1 cm x 7 cm fine fringed within 2 mm of edge.
Cut 1 cream strip 13 mm x 15 cm fine fringed within 2 mm of edge. Break strip into 30 5 mm pieces for stigmas.

Cut 30 dark green strips 2 mm x 7 cm. Break strip into 2 pieces one 4 cm the other 3 cm. See pattern 14.

Join all pieces following pattern 14 and coil from stigma end. When the glue is dry spread outer fringing. Apply a small amount of glue to the thin stigma fringing and twist gently into a spire.

14

Blossom Cups (Make 7)
Cut 7 dark green strips 2 mm x 15 cm. Coil to cup shape. Attach to 7 blossoms for side on mounting.

Buds (Make 10)
Cut 10 red-earth strips 2.5 mm x 12 cm. Coil to long cone. See pattern 15.

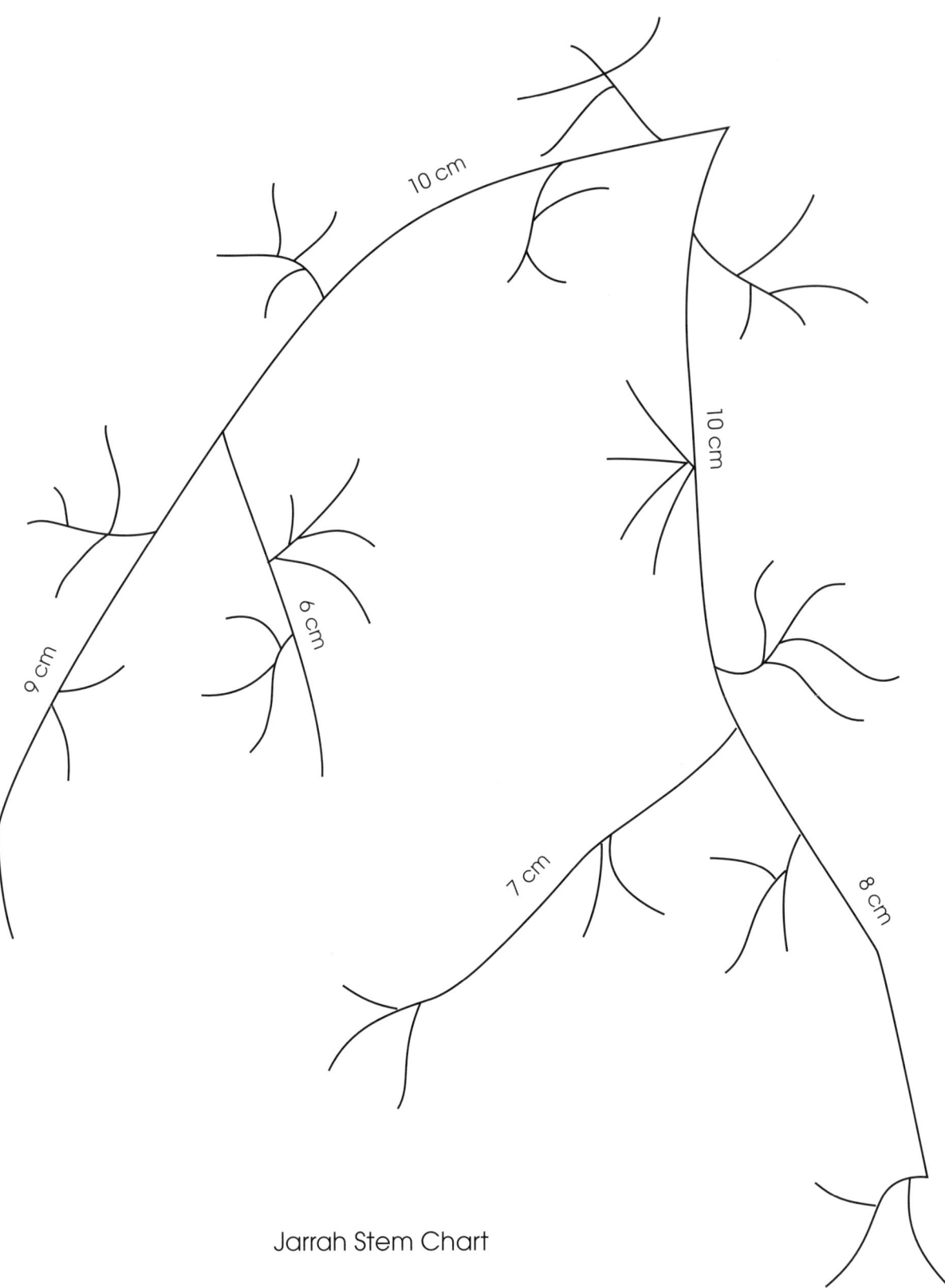

Jarrah Stem Chart

Cut 10 mid-green strips 2 mm x 12 cm. Coil to cup shape. See pattern 16.
Glue open ends, one of each colour.

15   16

Seed Pods (Make 7)

Cut 7 red-brown strips 2 mm x 12 cm. Coil to cup shape.
Cut red-brown 7 strips 2 mm x 12 cm. Coil using slotted tool to form a hole in the centre of the slightly concave disc. Fit disc on top of open cup to create a small central opening into the pod.

Leaves

Cut 1 dark green strip 10 cm x 18 cm. Coat one surface with 1 coat of PVA glue and allow to dry.
Cut 1 mid-green strip 10 cm x 18 cm. Glue to uncoated side of dark green strip.
Cut 5 from large pattern 17.
Cut 4 from smaller pattern 18.

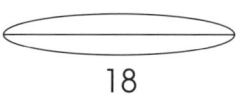

18

Emboss a deep prominent mid rib on the dark green side.
Cut 9 red-brown fine tapered strips 3 cm to 4 cm long. Position strip along groove of mid rib with thickest end extending 1 cm beyond leaf at attachment end.

Stems

MAIN STEM (4-LAYER THICKNESS)
Make 2 sets.
Cut 8 red-brown strips 2 mm x 10 cm and glue into layers.

SECONDARY STEMS (2 LAYER THICKNESS)
Cut 2 red-brown strips, 2 mm x 6 cm.
Cut 2 red-brown strips, 2 mm x 7 cm.
Cut 2 red-brown strips, 2 mm x 8 cm.
Cut 2 red brown strips, 2 mm x 9 cm.

FINE STEMS (1 THICKNESS)
Cut 47 red-brown strips, 2 mm x 1 cm to 3 cm long.
Each blossom, bud and pod will need a stem. Follow the chart or vary the size and position of each group as desired. The average group is 4.

Mounting

Position stems following the stem chart.
Position leaves as pictured or as desired.
Position bud and pod groups.
Position blossoms, some flat on backing, some at a slight angle on the end of fine stem and 7 cupped blossoms in a side-on position.

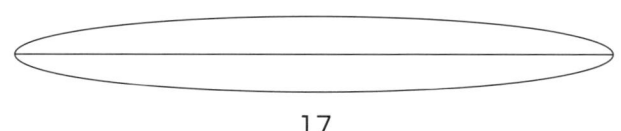

17

Jarrah — Miniature

(for gift tags 8 cm x 3.5 cm)

Materials

Canson papers

> Pale yellow (blossom fringing)
> Dark green (blossom centres and upper leaf)
> Red earth (buds)
> Mid green (bud cups and under leaf)
> Red brown (seed pods and stems)

Construction

Blossom (Make 3)

Cut 3 pale yellow strips 5 mm x 3 cm fine fringed.

Cut 3 pale yellow strips 8 mm x 5 mm fine fringed.

Cut 3 dark green strips 2 mm x 5 cm, break into 2 cm and 3 cm sections.

Join as shown, following pattern 19.

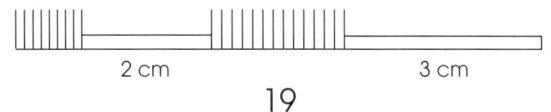

2 cm   3 cm

19

Bud (Make 2)

Cut 2 red-earth strips 2 mm x 8 cm to a cone shape. See pattern 20.

Cut 2 mid-green strips 2 mm x 8 cm to a cup shape. See pattern 21.

Glue open ends of each colour together.

Pods (Make 3)

Cut 3 red-brown strips 2 mm x 8 cm to a cup shape. See pattern 22.

20   21   22

Stems

Cut 1 red-brown strip 1 mm x 5 cm and break into suitable sizes

Leaf

Cut 3 from pattern 18.

Scraps of paper from the full size Jarrah leaves could be used, or prepare a 3 cm x 6 cm strip in the same way.

Emboss mid rib and attach a fine tapered strip to 1.5 cm long, extend 5 mm beyond leaf.

Attach pieces as shown or as desired.

SILVER MULLA MULLA
OR WHITE FOXTAIL

Ptilotus obovatus

An attractive and very prolific annual small shrub found in drier areas of Australia. It is less than 2 metres high and the woolly white hairs cover all but the green-brown leaves. This variety is lighter in colour than many of the other mulla mullas and will flower for most of the year.

Materials

Canson papers
> Pale pink (blossom centres)
>
> White (blossoms and stems)
>
> Coffee (leaves)

Scissors

Construction (needle tool)

5 flower heads of 12 blossoms in 2 sizes.
For each blossom:
Cut 1 pink strip 1 cm x 1.5 cm, fine fringe to within 3 mm of edge.
Cut 1 strip white, 1cm x 1.5cm, fine fringe to within 3 mm of edge.
Join fringed strips pink to white and coil from pink end.
Make 10 blossoms in this size for each flower head.
Larger blossoms:
Cut 1 pink strip 1.3 cm x 1.5 cm, fine fringe to within 3mm of edge.

Cut 1 white strip 1.3 cm x 1.5 cm, fine fringe to within 3mm of edge
Join as for smaller blossoms.
Only make 2 for each flower head.

Mounting Stem
Cut 1 white strip 1 cm x 4 cm and coil to a taped cone 2 cm long.

Attaching Blossoms
Using smaller blossoms first, position one blossom on the top of mounting stem then position 3 more below the first, evenly spacing them down the centre of the mounting stem. Take 3 more blossoms and position them at right angles to the first row — the 4th blossom should be the biggest. Repeat the same process on the other side of the centre row.
This should give the flower head a wider base so it looks like a cone.

Fuzzy Stem (Make 5)

Cut 1 white strip 7 mm x 10 cm, fine fringe to only 2 mm in depth. See pattern 23. Coil a 2 cm tapered cone. Coat the inside with glue to hold it firm before lifting fringing. When glue is dry, attach widest end over the base of the flower head.

Stems

Make 5 stems, each 5 layers thick.

Each stem is made of 4 straight strips and 1 fringed strip glued in layers.

Cut 1 white strip 5 mm x 12 cm with a very fine fringe to within 3 mm of edge, this is the centre strip.

Cut 4 white strips 3 mm x 12 cm.

To centre fringed strip, glue 2 straight strips on either side. Do not glue the fringing area.

Make 4 more stems in the same way but in different sizes: 10 cm, 9 cm, 7 cm, 5cm.

When strips are dry, gently spread the fringing, one tiny strand at a time, to alternate sides of the strip. See pattern 24.

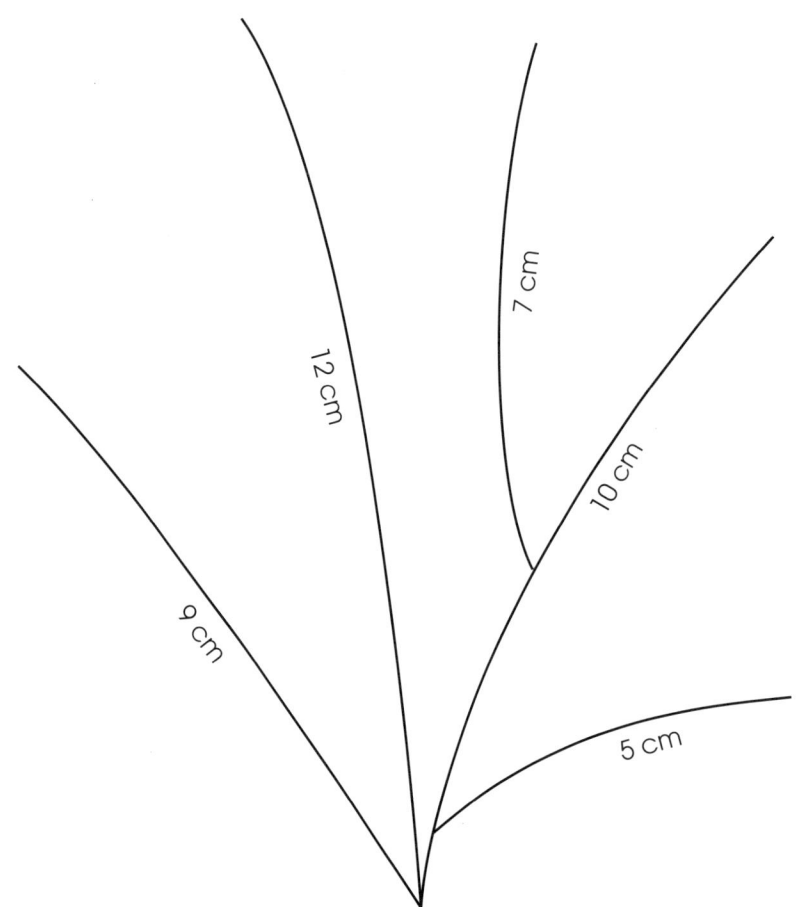

Silver Mulla Mulla Stem Chart

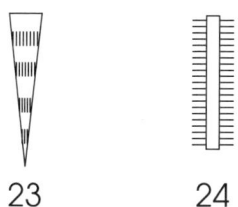

23   24

Leaves

Cut 6 in coffee from pattern 25

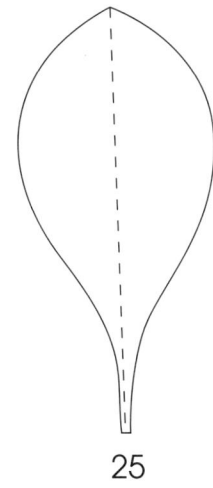

25

Mark centre mid rib and fold slightly, curve the narrow stem backwards for ease of attachment.

Mounting

Position stems as per stem chart.
Gently curve the fuzzy stem to position the flower head in same curve as stem.
When flower heads are dry, carefully spread the fringing to expose the pale pink centres. Position leaves in pairs against the sides of the stems. Apply a little glue to the underside of the leaves to hold them in place.

Silver Mulla Mulla or White Foxtail — Miniature

(for gift tags 8 cm x 3.5 cm)

Materials

Canson papers
    Pale pink (blossom centres)
    White (blossom and stems)
    Coffee (leaves)
Scissors

Construction

Blossoms (Make 12)

For each blossom:
Cut 1 pink strip 7 mm x 1 cm, fine fringe to within 2 mm of edge.
Cut 1 white strip 7 mm x 1 cm, fine fringe to within 2 mm of edge.
Join together and coil from pink end.

Stem

Cut 1 white strip 3 mm x 2 cm, fine fringe.

Leaves

Cut 7 coffee leaves from pattern 26.

26

Mounting

Follow the photograph or position as desired.

ORANGE IMMORTELLE

Waitzia acuminata

A small herb that grows in dry sandy places. If conditions are right, it will flower in winter and in spring each year. The bright yellow and orange heads are really eye catching. It belongs to the everlasting daisy family, but its flowers are cone shaped not flat. The flowers can also be used in dried floral arrangements.

Materials

Canson papers
  Yellow (petals)
  Orange (petal fringing and buds)
  Pale green (leaves, stems and calyx)
White photocopy paper A4 (internal padding)
Embossing tool for mid ribs
Round ended tool for pressing petal shaping
Soft eraser to press into for petal shaping

Construction (needle and slotted tool)

Blossoms (yellow — slotted tool)
Make 9 blossoms. For each blossom:
Cut 1 yellow strip 1 cm x 30 cm. Cut petal shapes as shown in pattern 27.
Cut 1 yellow strip 2 cm x 5 cm. Cut petal shapes as shown in pattern 28.
Press centre of each petal to concave.
Cut 1 white strip in copy paper 1 cm x 30 cm. Join strips as shown in pattern 29.
Slowly tight coil from the 5 cm yellow strip end with petals curving in and over each other, tapering slightly as you go. Straight coil white strip onto the uncut section of the 5 cm yellow strip. When you reach the 30 cm yellow strip, spot glue as you go, taper coils slowly upwards, make 3 or 4 straight rounds at the middle then continue to taper to the end. Take care as there will be a gap between the white centre and the outer petal strip at the top. Glue the last 2 rounds completely and allow to dry. Remove tool carefully.

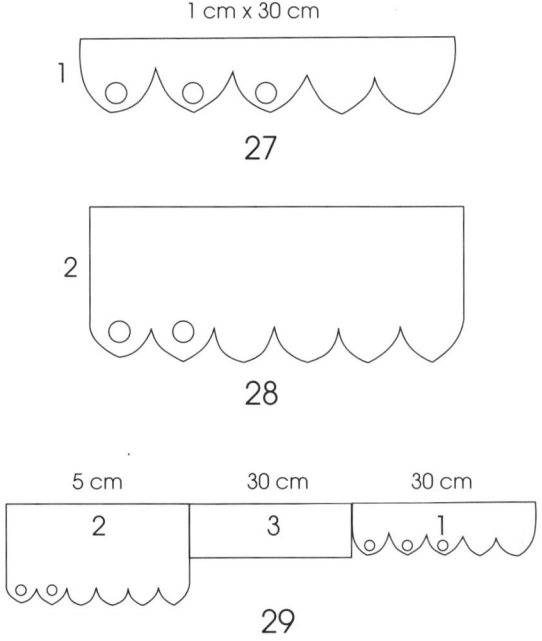

Blossom Fringing
(orange — needle tool)

FOR EACH BLOSSOM:

Cut 1 orange strip 2 cm x 5 cm. Fine fringe to within 3 mm of edge. Cut a wavy edge then tight coil. See pattern 30.

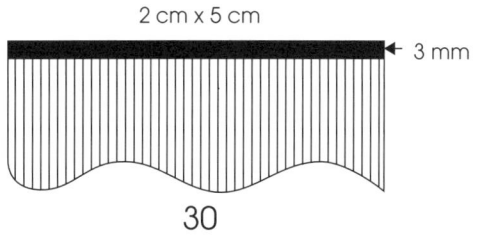

30

Spread fringing at right angles. See pattern 31. Apply glue to top edge of outer yellow petals and gently press fringing over the glue and down over the petals, forming a cap that should sit up giving a rounded appearance to the top of the yellow petals. See pattern 32.

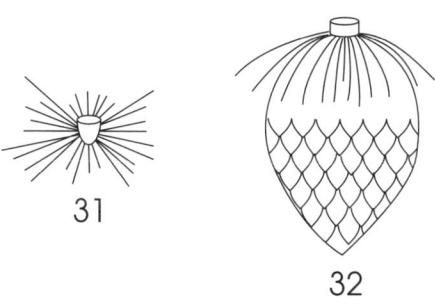

31

32

Calyx (pale green — slotted tool)

FOR EACH BLOSSOM (SEE PATTERN 33):

Cut 1 pale green strip following the pattern, 1 cm for 1.5 cm then 5 mm for 9.5 cm.

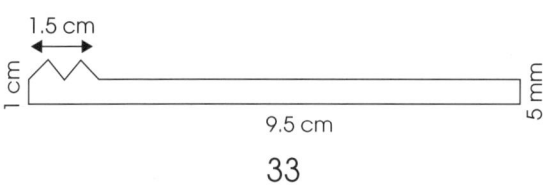

33

Coil to long cone up to 2 cm. When dry, bend points backwards and glue open end down over the knob of the orange fringing. Glue points down into fringing. When dry, curve calyx cone slightly to continue curve of stems when mounting.

Buds (Make 2)
(orange — needle tool)

Cut 2 orange strips 1 cm x 6 cm, fine fringe to 3 mm of edge. Tight coil to a slight taper.
Cut 2 tapered orange strips 5 mm to 1.5 cm x 6 cm. Fine fringe to 3 mm. Tight coil from widest end, open to right angles.
Glue open right angle pieces over open end of each of the slightly tapered pieces.

Bud Calyx
(pale green — slotted tool)

Cut 2 from the blossom calyx pattern, coil and attach in the same way as for the full blossom.

Leaves
(pale green — slotted tool)

Cut 16 leaves from the larger pattern. See pattern 34.
Cut 6 leaves from the smaller pattern. See pattern 35.

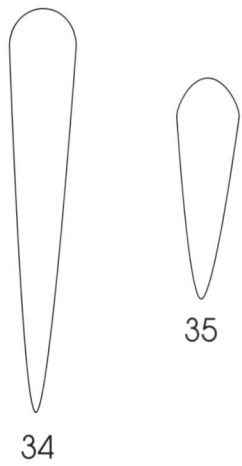

35

34

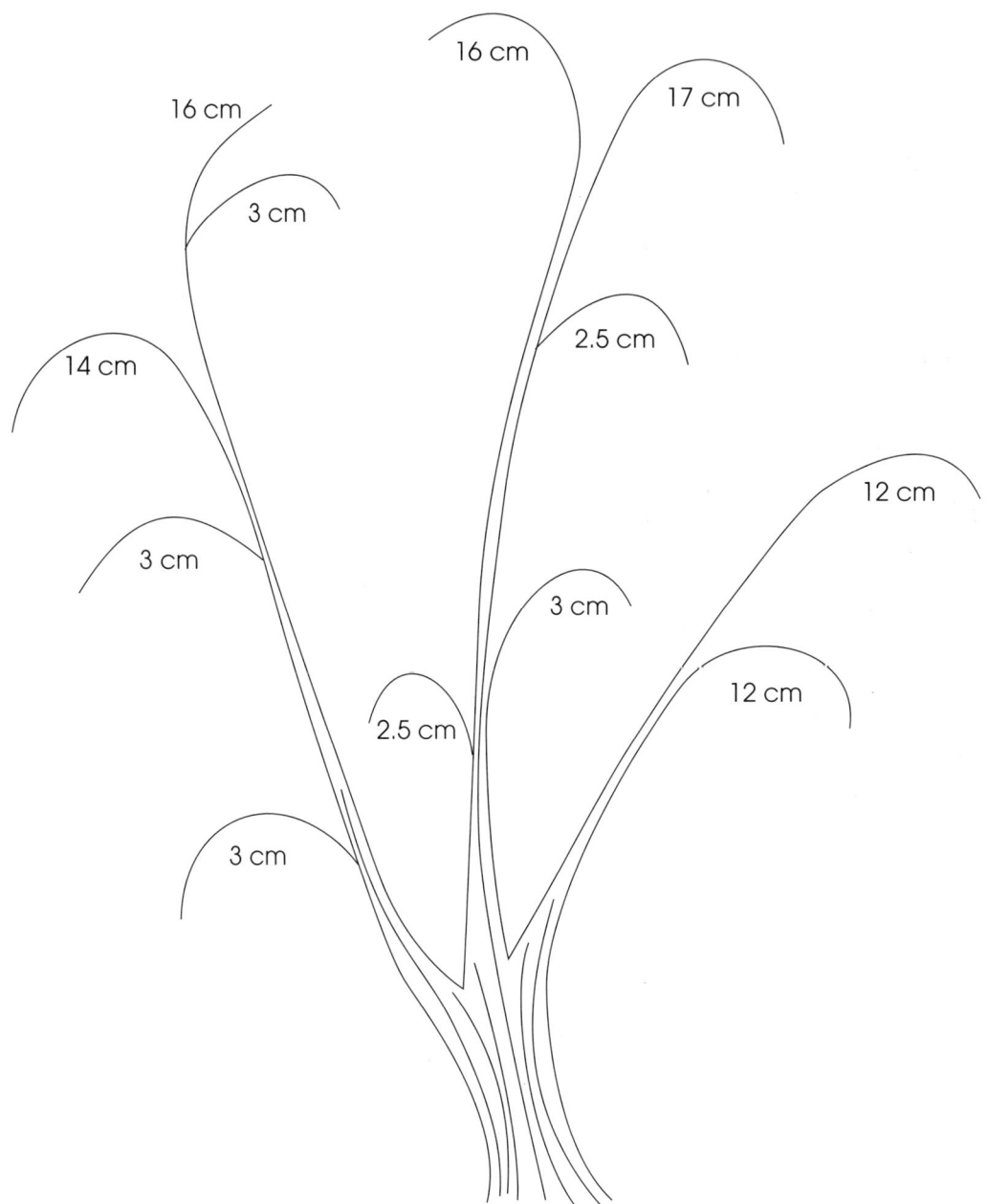

16 cm

16 cm

17 cm

3 cm

2.5 cm

14 cm

3 cm

12 cm

3 cm

2.5 cm

12 cm

3 cm

Orange Immortelle Stem Chart

Emboss centre mid rib. Using slotted tool, gently curl leaf edges under slightly.

Stems

All are pale green, attached on edge. Follow stem chart.

Cut 1 strip 3 mm x 17 cm, curve top 2 cm.

Cut 2 strips 3 mm x 16 cm, curve top 2 cm.

Cut 1 strip 3 mm x 14 cm, curve top 2 cm.

Cut 2 strips 3 mm x 12 cm, curve top 2 cm.

Fill in spaces between these stems as desired with strips the same width and length.

Secondary Stems (all pale green)

Cut 4 strips 3 mm x 3 cm curve.

Cut 2 strips 3 mm x 2.5 cm curve.

Attach as per stem chart.

Mounting

Attach all stems and allow to dry.

Position all blossoms first, then position buds.

Curve leaves backwards and attach by 5 mm of the narrow end to the side of the stem.

Orange Immortelle — Miniature

(for gift tag 8 cm x 3.5 cm)

Materials

Canson papers

    Yellow (petals)

    Orange (petal fringing and buds)

    Pale green (leaves, stems and calyx)

Blossoms (yellow — slotted tool)

Cut 1 yellow strip 5 mm x 8.5 cm. Cut petals following pattern 36.

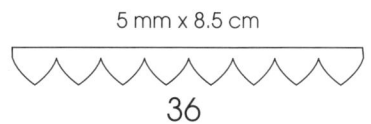

5 mm x 8.5 cm

36

Tight coil, tapered but fat in the middle.

Fringing (orange — needle tool)

Cut 1 orange strip 1 cm x 2 cm. Fine fringe along 2 cm edge to within 2 mm of edge. Tight coil and spread fringing. Attach as for full size blossom.

Bud (orange — needle tool)

Cut 1 orange strip 4 mm tapered to 8 mm x 4 cm. Fine fringe to 2 mm of edge. Tight coil from widest end.

Calyx for blossom and buds (pale green — slotted tool)

1 pale green strip 3 mm x 7 cm coil to a 7 mm cone.

Glue open ends over fringing knobs.

Leaves

Cut 3 from pattern 37.

37

Mounting

Follow the photograph or position as desired.

BLUE PINCUSHION

Brunonia australis

A pretty annual herb that grows to 1 metre high. It is a species unique to Australia. The bright blue flower heads appear from late winter to early summer. Each flower cluster has its own long stalk with a circle of broad leaves at its base. This small plant grows in mainly dry areas but will adapt to home gardens as a rockery plant in drier parts of Australia.

Materials

Canson papers
    Bright blue (flowers)
    Pale green (stem cup, stems and leaves)
Gold dimensional paint for stigma tip
Scissors
Embossing tool

Construction (needle tool)

Make 4 flower clusters each consisting of 18 flowers — 72 flowers in bright blue in total. For each flower make:

Stigma
Cut 1 bright blue strip 1.5 mm x 1.5 cm.
Cut 1 bright blue strip 1.5 mm x 1 cm.
Join the 1 cm at right angles to 1.5 cm strip. Leave a 4 mm length at the top. See pattern 38.

Petals
Cut 5 bright blue petals for each flower (360 petals), using pattern 39.

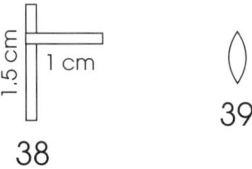

Position evenly along the 1 cm strip. See pattern 40.

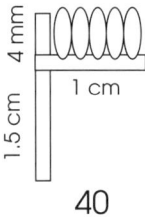

When dry, tight coil from stigma end of the 1.5 cm strip. Gently spread petals out at right angles and ease into a 5 point star. Using gold dimensional paint, dip the 4 mm tip of the stigma and allow to dry, then close petals to allow for attachment for quilling the centre.

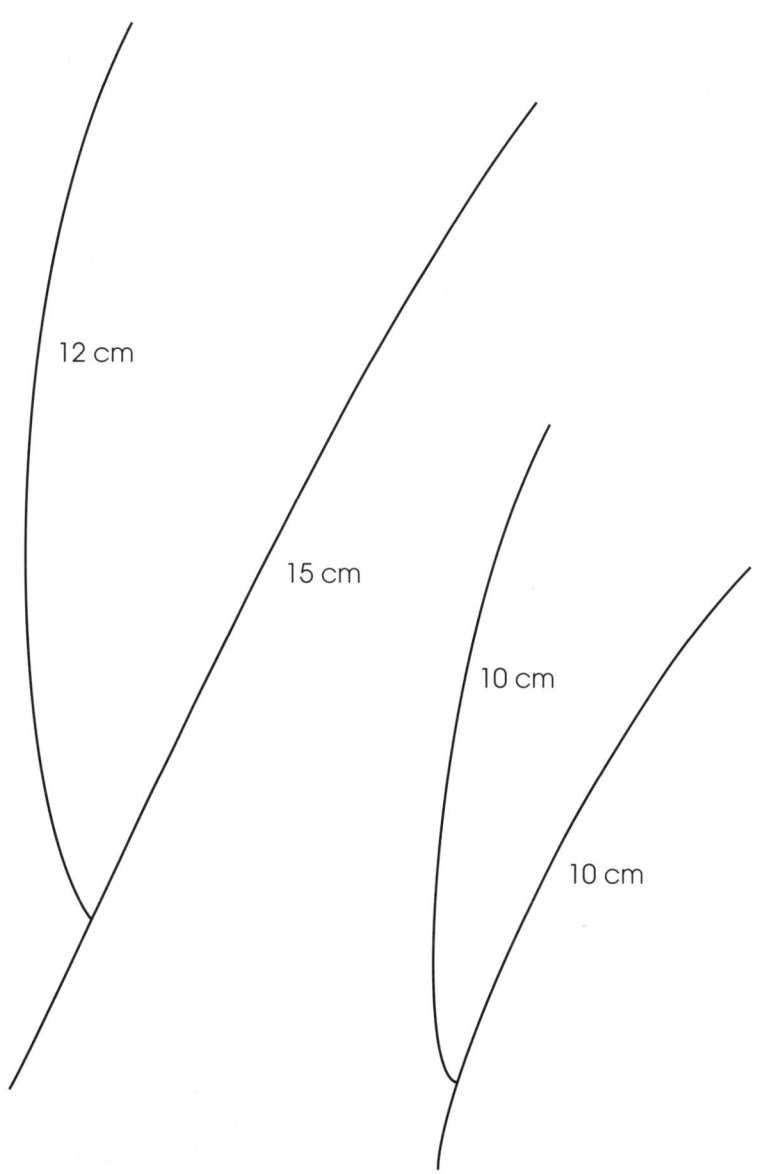

12 cm

15 cm

10 cm

10 cm

Blue Pincushion Stem Chart

Centre

Cut 1 bright blue strip 2 mm x 12 cm.

Leave 1cm at each end free of flowers.

Attach 18 flowers evenly along the rest of the strip.

When dry, tight coil to a wide short cone. See pattern 41.

Stem Cups (Make 4)

Cut 1 pale green strip 2 mm x 15 cm.

Cut 6 pale green claws 1 cm long. Follow pattern 42.

41   42   43

Position claws evenly on the last 2 cm of the green 15 cm strip.

Tight coil from the free end to a pointed cup with claws pointing up all around. See pattern 43.

Bend claws out to allow the open end of the flower centre to be glued inside the green stem cup. Bring claws up amongst the flowers.

Stems

Cut 1 light green stem 4 mm tapered to 6 mm x 15 cm.

Cut 1 light green stem 4 mm tapered to 6 mm x 12 cm.

Cut 2 light green stems 4 mm tapered to 6 mm x 10 cm.

Fold evenly lengthways.

Curve slightly.

Leaves

Cut 9 light green leaves from pattern 44.

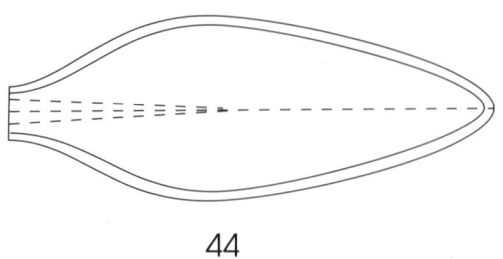

44

Heavily emboss centre midrib and fold slightly lengthways.

Fold 1.5 mm of leaf margin back slightly to give a curved under edge.

Mounting

Position stems as per stem chart.

Position flower heads with the bottom tip of stem cup inside 4 mm end of stem. Glue a section of the wider part of the stem cup to the backing. Do not glue any flowers to the backing. When dry, gently ease the flowers down between claws, opening each flower on the bottom row to partly cover the stem cup. Working one row at a time, bring each flower forward and open it into a star until all flowers are open and the blossom looks like a ball.

Position leaves as photographed or as desired to create clusters at the base of the stems.

Blue Pincushion — Miniature

(for gift tag 8cm x 3.5cm)

Materials

Canson papers
Bright blue (flowers)
Pale green (leaves)

Construction

Make 12 flowers. For each make:

Stigma

Cut 2 bright blue strips 1.5 mm x 1 cm.
Join at right angles. See pattern 45.

Petals

Cut 5 petals for each flower (60 petals in total) in bright blue. See pattern 46.
Follow the full size pattern for the petals.

Leaves

Cut 8 green leaves. See pattern 47.
Treat the same as for the full size leaves.

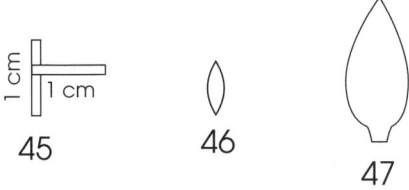

45   46   47

Mounting

Follow the instructions below or make up your own.

Card 1

Make a small cluster of 5 flowers.
Cut 1 light green strip 1.5 mm x 2.5 cm.
Attach flowers along this strip leaving 5 mm free one end and 7 mm free the other end.
Coil to a cup shape working from 5 mm end.
Cut 1 light green strip 1.5 mm x 1.5 cm for a stem (see photograph).
Attach stem to card, then attach the green cup (not flowers) to the tip of the stem.
Position 3 leaves at the base of the stem.

Card 2

Attach 3 flowers by their bright blue stems to one corner of the card, then fan 3 leaves from the flower stems.

Card 3

Attach 3 flowers by overlapping their bright blue stems at one corner. Snip the bright blue stem from 1 flower and position the flower straight down on top of the other 3 stems.
Attach 2 leaves.

WILD ORANGE OR NATIVE POMEGRANATE

Capparis mitchellii

T his small tree or fairly large shrub is found in a wide variety of climates. Moist coastal areas to the arid inland can all boast of its presence. Its adaptability has allowed this plant, with a spectacular 6 cm creamy flower, to become widespread. Flowering can occur any time during the year. As a bush-tucker food, it is relished for its passionfruit-like seed pod. A number of different varieties are used in cultivated gardens along with a few introduced types of the same species.

Materials

Canson papers
    Pale lemon (petals, stamen and stigma)
    Mid green (bud covers, tip of stigma and leaves)
    Mid brown (calyx , stems, seed pod and spent stigma)
Scissors
Soft eraser to press on
Round ended tool for pressing
Gold dimensional paint for stamen tips

Construction (needle tool)

Blossoms (Make 3)

For each blossom make:

PETALS
Cut 4 pale lemon petals from pattern 48. Press into a cupped shape where indicated on pattern 49. Use soft eraser and round ended tool. The petal should have a crumpled edge.

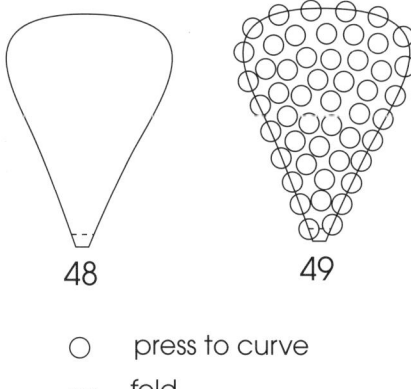

48   49

○   press to curve
---   fold

BUD COVERS
2 for each blossom.
Cut 2 mid-green bud covers from pattern 50. Curve the same way as the petals following pattern 51.

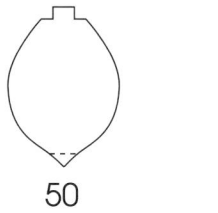
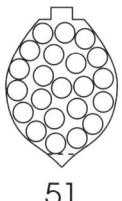

50   51

STIGMA

Cut 1 pale lemon strip 1.5 mm x 9 cm. Fold in half and glue.

This should make a strong 4.5 cm strip.

STIGMA TIP

Cut 1 mid-green strip 1.5 mm x 2.5 cm. Coil into tapered cone to 5 mm.

Fit the open end of the cone over the folded end of the stigma.

STAMEN

Cut 1 pale lemon strip 4 cm x 12 cm. Fine fringe along 12 cm length to within 3 mm of edge. Brush tips of the stamen with gold dimensional paint and allow to dry.

Before coiling the stamen, attach the bottom end of the stigma parallel with the last fringe at the end you will coil from. Tight coil.

Attach petals evenly by gluing the last 3 mm of the thin end of the petal around the 3 mm section of the fringing.

Attach the bud covers by gluing the last 2 mm at the pointed end of the cover, opposite each other and between petals on the 3 mm section.

Spread the bud covers, petals and fringing open on two of the blossoms.

Leave the third blossom unopened.

CALYX

Cut 1 mid-brown strip 2 mm x 20 cm. Coil to stemmed cup. See pattern 52.

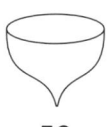

52

Attach open end of cup to the base of the 3 mm fringed section.

Buds (Make 3)

Cut 2 mid-green strips 2 mm x 35 cm, tight coil to cup shape.

Make one with a pointed end and the other a smooth cup and join open ends together. See pattern 53.

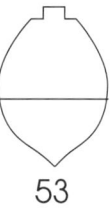

53

Seed Pod

Cut 2 mid-brown strips 2 mm x 70 cm. Tight coil to deep wide cup shape.

Make one with a pointed end, the other a smooth cup, and join open ends together. See pattern 54.

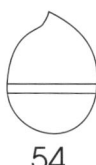

54

Spent Stigma

Cut 1 mid-brown strip 1.5 mm x 10 cm. Fold in half and glue.

Cut 1 mid-brown strip 1.5 mm x 2.5 cm coil to a tapered cone to 5 mm long.

Glue open end of cone over tip of folded strip.

Leaves (Make 8)

Cut mid-green leaves from pattern 55. Emboss centre mid rib.

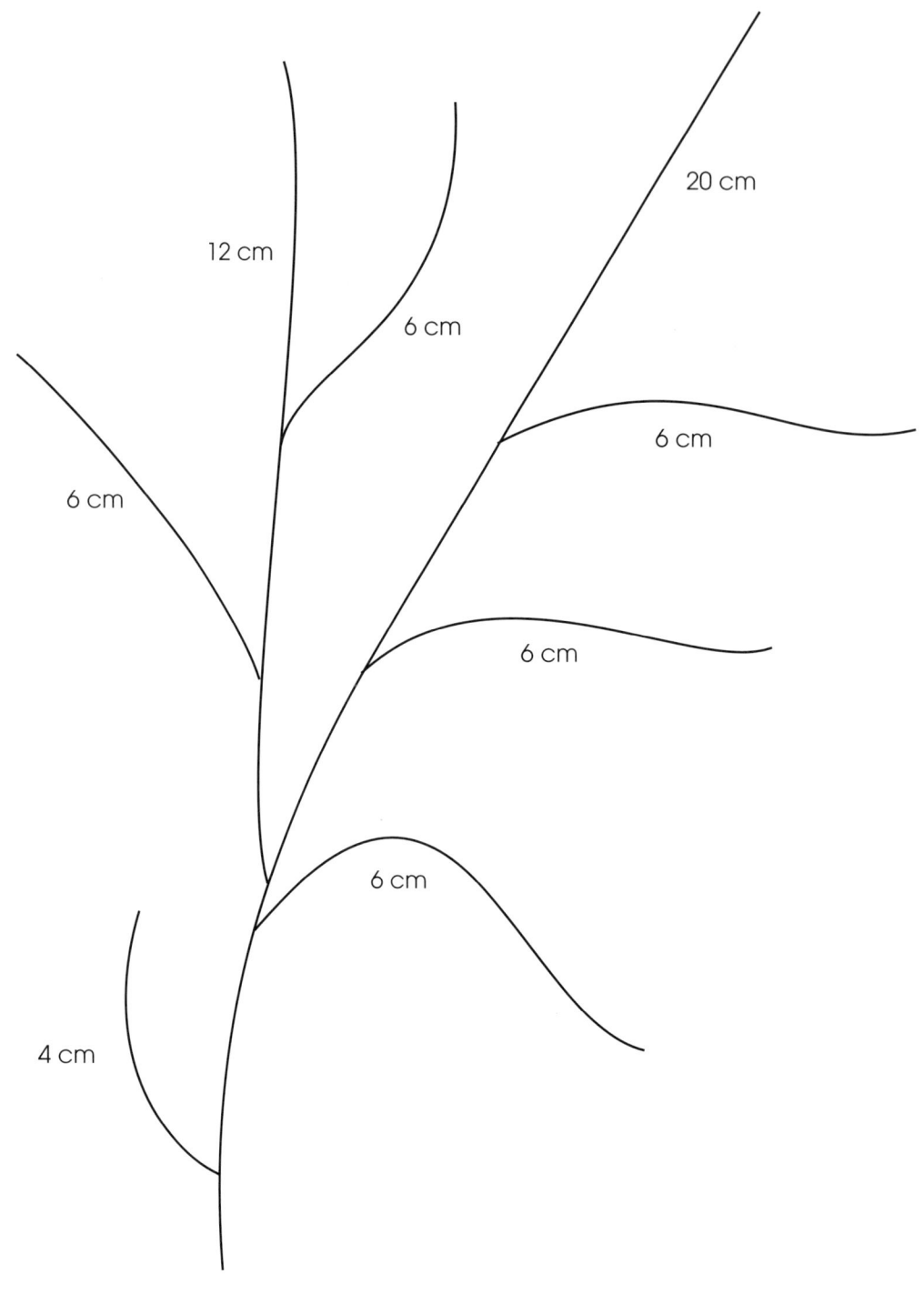

12 cm

20 cm

6 cm

6 cm

6 cm

6 cm

6 cm

4 cm

Wild Orange Stem Chart

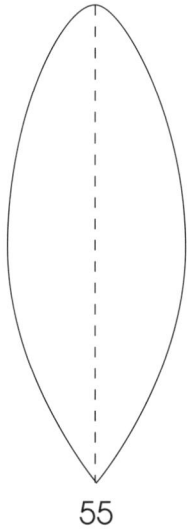

55

Cut 8 mid-brown strips 1.5 mm to very fine tip 7.5 cm long.

Glue brown strip along mid rib line with the 1.5 mm end protruding about 1 cm beyond leaf for attaching to stems.

Stems (laminated)

MAIN STEM (6-LAYER THICKNESS)

Cut 6 mid-brown strips 2 mm x 20 cm. Glue to a thick stem.

SECONDARY STEMS (4-LAYER THICKNESS)

Cut 4 mid-brown strips 2 mm x 12 cm to make 1 stem.

Cut 20 mid-brown strips 2 mm x 6 cm to make 5 stems.

Cut 4 mid-brown strips 2 mm x 4 cm to make 1 stem.

Mounting

Following the stem chart, position stems.

Attach the blossoms as shown.

Attach the buds at an angle so they touch the stems.

Attach the seed pod at an angle to touch the stem.

Attach the leaves by the brown strips, mostly alternately down stems.

Attach the spent stigma so it overlaps a leaf. This will make it easier to see.

Wild Orange — Miniature

(for gift tags 8 cm x 3.5 cm)

Materials

Canson papers

    Pale lemon (stigma, stamen and petals)

    Mid green (bud, bud cups and leaves)

    Mid brown stems (leaf vein and seed pod)

Construction

Blossoms (Make 3)

For each make:

PETALS

Cut 4 pale lemon petals, from pattern 56.

Press into a cup shape.

Bud Covers, cut 2 mid-green, from pattern 57.

Press into a cup shape.

56   57   58

STIGMA

Cut 1 pale lemon strip 1.5 mm x 2 cm. See pattern 58. Tip with green dimensional paint.

Or

Cut 1 mid-green strip 1 mm x 1 cm. Join at right angles to one end of lemon strip. Coil the green strip around the tip of the lemon strip.

STAMEN

Cut 1 pale lemon strip 1.5 mm x 4.5 cm. Fine fringe to within 2 mm of edge.
Brush tips of fringing with gold dimensional paint.
When dry, attach the stigma parallel with fringing at one end and tight coil from that end.
Attach the petals evenly spaced to the 2 mm uncut section of the fringing strip (stamen).
Attach the bud covers opposite each other between the petals.

CALYX

Cut 2 mid-brown strips 2 mm x 12 cm. Coil to a stemmed cup.
Attach to 2 blossoms.

LEAVES

Cut 2 cut from pattern 59. Emboss mid rib.
Cut 2 mid-brown strips 1 mm to very fine point x 3 cm long.
Glue the brown strip down the mid rib.

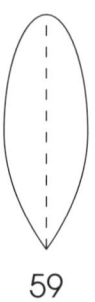

59

SEED POD

Cut 1 mid-brown strip 2 mm x 12 cm. Coil to round bottom cup shape.

BUD

Cut 1 mid-green strip 2 mm x 12 cm. Coil to cup shape with small stem.

STEMS

Cut 3 mid-brown stems 1 mm x 1 cm. Glue onto card by the edge.
Cut 1 mid-brown strip 1 mm x 2.5 cm. Glue onto card by the edge.

Mounting

Mount as shown in the photograph or as desired.

Kangaroo Apple (page 8)

Jarrah (page 13)

Silver Mulla Mulla or White Foxtail (page 17)

Kangaroo Apple Miniature
(page 11)

Jarrah Miniature (page 16)

Silver Mulla Mulla or White
Foxtail Miniature (page 19)

Orange Immortelle (page 20)

Poached Egg Daisy (page 48)

Round-Leaved Parakeelya (page 52)

Large-Flowered Guichenotia
Miniature (page 47)

Poached Egg Daisy Miniature
(page 51)

Round-Leaved Parakeelya
Miniature (page 55)

GIDGEE

Acacia cambagei

Most people think of wattles as bright yellow balls of fluffy colour, which appear in spring. This wattle is a little different being almost white and flowering in autumn and into winter. A small multi-stem tree from the drier areas of our vast country, it is often found growing in the company of mallee trees in what is termed 'mallee scrub'.

Materials

Canson papers
    Off white (flowers)
    Dark green (leaves and stems)
Scissors
Embossing tool

Construction (needle tool)

Blossoms

Make 37 large blossoms. For each blossom:
Cut 1 off-white strip 1 cm x 8 cm, fine fringe to within 2 mm of edge. Tight coil and spread fringing out and down to make a half ball shape.
Make 11 small blossoms. For each blossom:
Cut 1 off-white strip 6 mm x 5 cm, fine fringe to within 3 mm of edge. Spread fringing.
Make 6 buds. For each bud:
Cut 1 off-white strip 4 mm x 3 cm. Tight coil.

Flower Stems (about 50)

Use dark green scraps from leaf cuttings to cut strips 1 mm to 1.5 mm wide and 1cm to 2 cm long. Attach these to the base of some blossoms and buds but only just before mounting. See pattern 60.

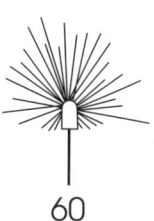

60

Main Stems (4-layer thickness)

Make 3 stems laminated in sets of 4.
Cut 12 dark green strips 2 mm x 15 cm. Glue in layers and allow to dry.
Make 3 stems laminated in sets of 4.
Cut 4 dark green strips 2 mm x 15 cm. Glue in layers and allow to dry.

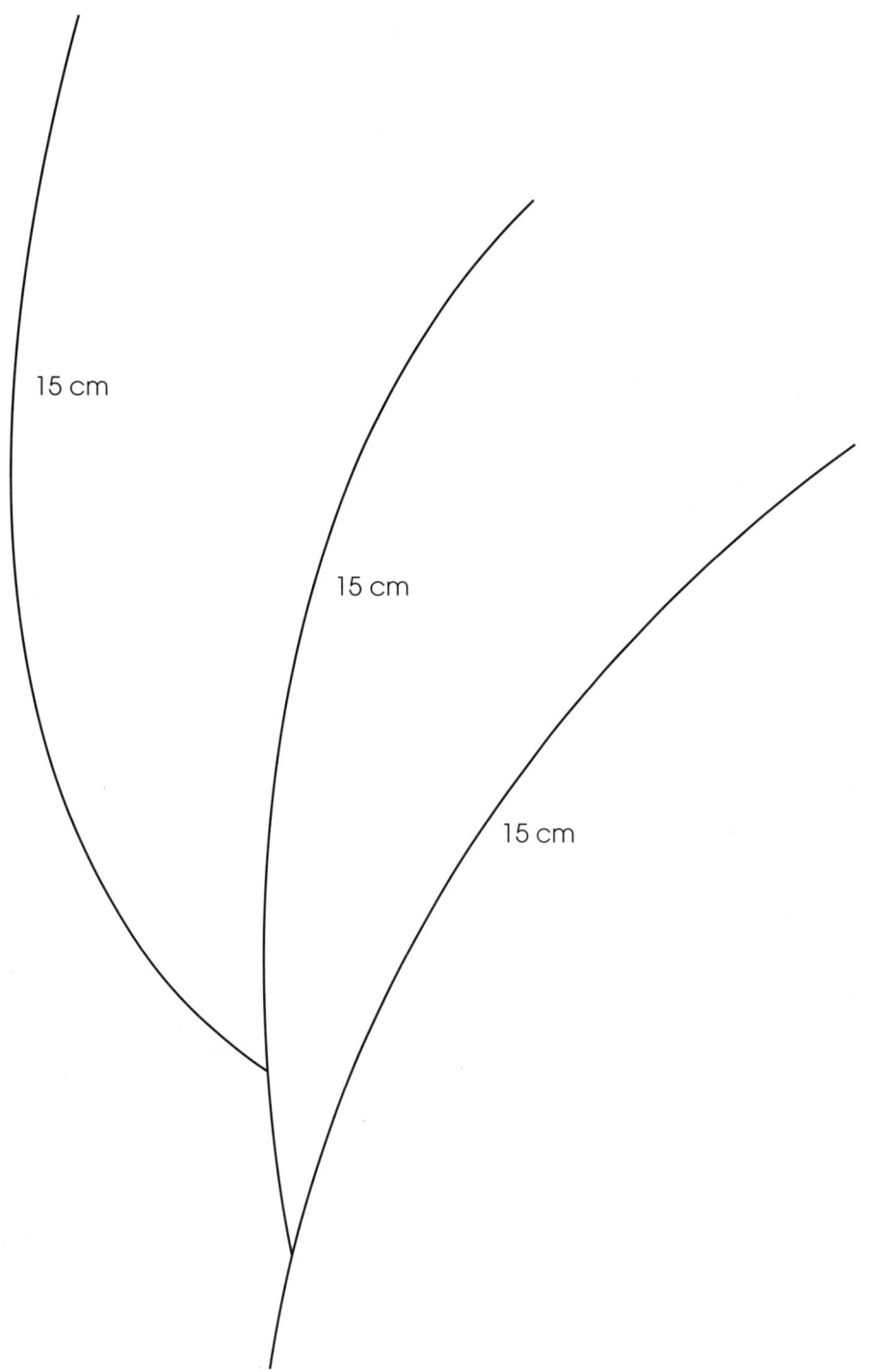

15 cm

15 cm

15 cm

Gidgee Stem Chart

Leaves

Make in dark green with 3 ribs down each leaf.

Cut 7 large leaves from pattern 61.

Cut 7 small leaves from pattern 62.

Fold slightly along centre mid rib.

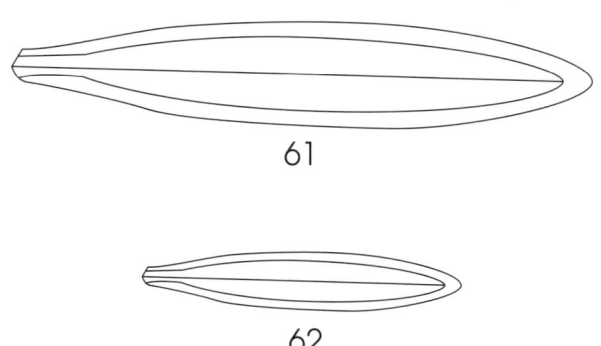

61

62

Mounting

Position the main stems following the chart.

Position leaves as pictured or as desired but remember leaves grow alternately down the stem.

Now decide which blossoms have stems and which do not. Do a 'dry run' to see how the blossoms will fit in the leaf axis. When you are satisfied with the layout, glue all the pieces in place. Remember to position the smallest at the top and the largest further down.

Gidgee — Miniature

(for gift tags 8 cm x 3.5 cm)

Materials

Canson papers

    Off white (flowers)

    Dark green (leaves)

For 3 cards you will need:

Larger Blossom (Make 6)

Cut 1 off-white strip 5 mm x 3 cm, fine fringe to within 2 mm of edge.

Tight coil and spread fringing.

Smaller Blossom (Make 5)

Cut 1 off-white strip 3 mm x 3 cm, fine fringe to within 1.5 mm of edge.

Tight coil and spread fringing.

Buds (Make 3)

Cut 1 off-white strip 2 mm x 2 cm. Tight coil.

Blossom Stems

Cut 11 dark green stems 1 mm x 1 cm to 2 cm depending on application.

Leaves

Cut 3 dark green leaves from pattern 63.

Emboss 3 ribs and bend lengthways slightly.

Mounting as picture or as desired.

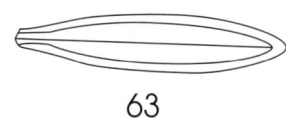

63

DESERT FRINGE MYRTLE

Calytrix longiflora

This delightful small plant is only one species of a family that grows to 2 metres and can be found in many areas of Australia, from the Simpson Desert to coastal plains and open forests. Flower colours range from white to pinks to purples. This is a lovely plant that deserves to be part of many native home gardens.

Materials

Canson papers

    Violet (stamen, petals, long fine fringe and short stems)

    Yellow (stamen)

    Mid green (stems and clasping leaves)

Scissors

Eraser

Fine knitting needle or wire

Construction (needle tool)

Blossoms (Make 14)

For each flower:

Cut 5 violet petals from pattern 64.

Using an eraser to press on, concave full length of each petal.

64

Stamen

Cut 1 violet strip 1 cm long 2 cm high. Cut off a tapered section then fine fringe to within 3mm. See pattern 65.

Cut 1 yellow strip 1 cm long 2 cm high. Treat the same as for violet strip.

Join strips as shown in pattern 66.

Tight coil from yellow end.

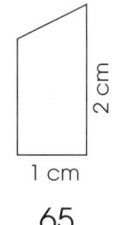

65

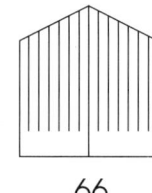

66

Long fine fringe strip

Cut 5 violet strips 2 mm to fine point 3 to 4 cm long. See pattern 67.

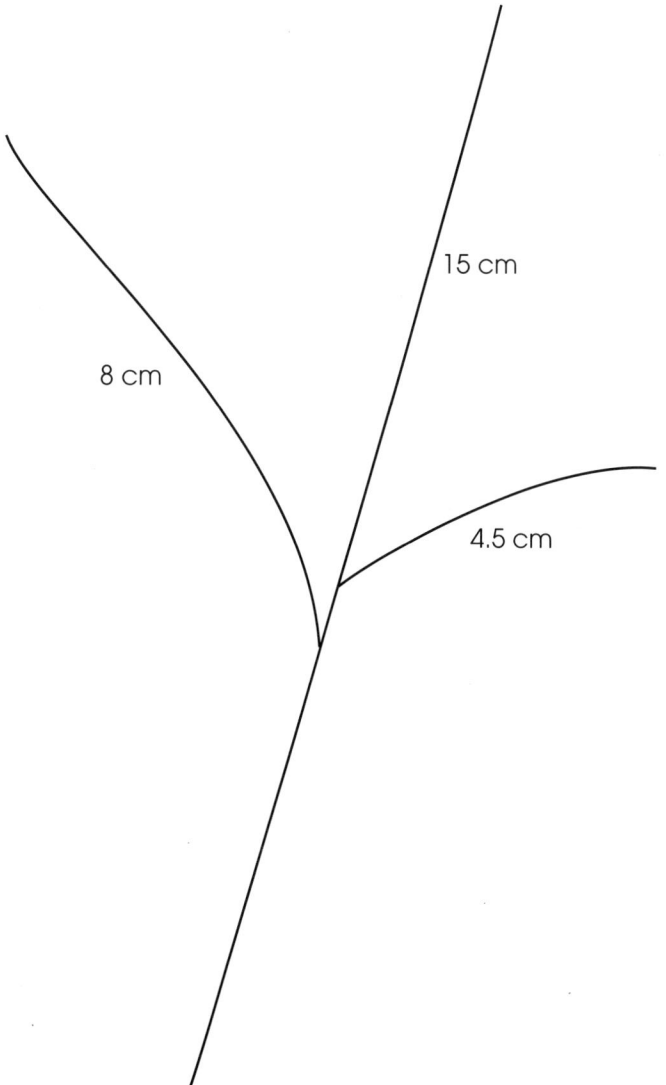

8 cm

15 cm

4.5 cm

Desert Fringe Myrtle Stem Chart

2 mm

67

Short stem

Cut 1 violet strip 3 mm x 5 cm. Coil to tapered cone to 1 cm long.

Take the fringed stamen centre and position the petals evenly (concave face in) to the 3 mm uncut section of the centre. Allow glue to dry. Position the long fine fringe strips by the widest end, to the 3 mm uncut section of the centre, one between each petal. Allow glue to dry. See pattern 68.

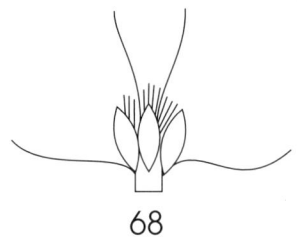

68

Glue the widest open end of the short stem cone over the 3 mm uncut end of the centre. When dry, spread the petals at right angles to the stamen. Spread the stamen centre to show the yellow throat of the blossom.

Stems and Leaves

These are all in one. As the leaves hug the stem very closely, it would be very time consuming to attach them individually, so I have designed a twisted strip which gives a similar effect.

Cut each strip in zig-zag pattern. See pattern 69.

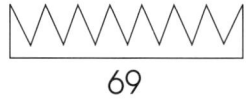

69

Twist carefully around a very fine knitting needle or a 1 mm thick wire.

Cut 1 mid-green strip 7 mm x 19 cm. Twist to 15 cm.

Cut 1 mid-green strip 7 mm x 10 cm. Twist to 8 cm.

Cut 1 mid-green strip 7 mm x 7 cm. Twist to 4.5 cm.

Mounting

Position the stems following the stem chart. Do not flatten stems but allow the points to sit naturally when gluing.

Position blossoms in groups at the tops of each stem.

Desert Fringe Myrtle — Miniature

(for gift tags 8 cm x 3.5 cm)

70

Materials

Canson papers
  Violet (long fringe and short stems)
  Yellow (stamen)

Construction

Flowers (Make 6)
For each flower:

CENTRE
Cut 1 yellow piece 1 cm x 1 cm, fine fringe to within 2 mm of edge and tight coil.

PETALS
Cut 5 violet petals from pattern 70.

FINE FRINGING
Cut 5 fine tapered strips 1.5 cm long.

SHORT STEM
Cut 1 violet strip 3 mm x 2 cm. Coil to tapered cone 7 mm long.
Attach the petals as for full size blossom but overlap the petals slightly for a neat fit.
Make 1 blossom with short stem.
Make 5 blossoms without short stems.

Mounting

As in the photograph or as desired.

PITURI

Duboisia hopwoodii

A multi-branched shrub that grows up to 5 metres tall. It has purple-striped white trumpet flowers that are clustered in groups of 3 or 4 blossoms. Flowering time is spring and summer. Black juicy berries from the plant were used by Aborigines as a medicine. This plant grows best in the sandy soil of the inland areas.

Materials

Canson papers
>   White (blossoms and buds)
>   Yellow (stamen)
>   Black (berries)
>   Mid green (calyx, leaves and some stems)
>   Mid brown (main stem and one small stem)

Scissors

Fine purple marker or fine purple pen

Embossing tool for mid ribs

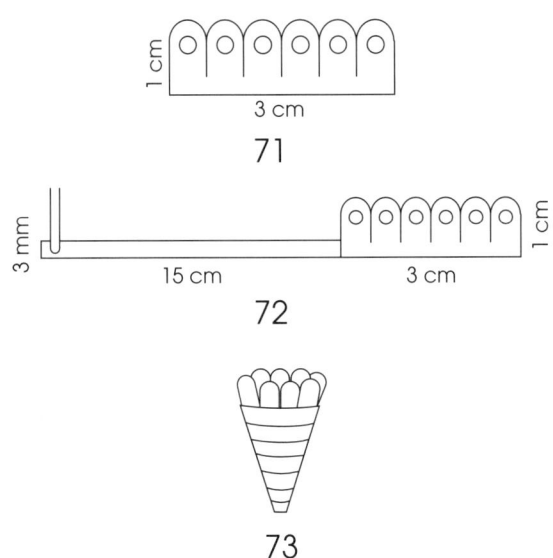

Construction (needle tool)

Blossoms (Make 13, or if you don't like 13 make 14)

For each blossom:

Cut 1 white strip 3 mm x 15 cm.

Cut 2 yellow strips 1 mm to a fine point 1.5 cm long.

Cut 1 white strip 1 cm x 3 cm. Cut petal pattern. Mark the inside of each petal with a few random purple lines and press O points from back of petal. See pattern 71.

Join these pieces as shown. See pattern 72.

Coil from the stamen end to form a long cone to 1.5 cm long. See pattern 73.

Glue the entire bottom edge of the petal section to the top edge of the cone.

When glue is dry, bend petals outwards to expose the yellow stamen and purple stripes.

Calyx (one for each blossom)

Cut 1 mid-green strip 2 mm x 5 cm. Coil to a tapered cone to 6 mm long.

Glue the open end over the bottom tip of each blossom.

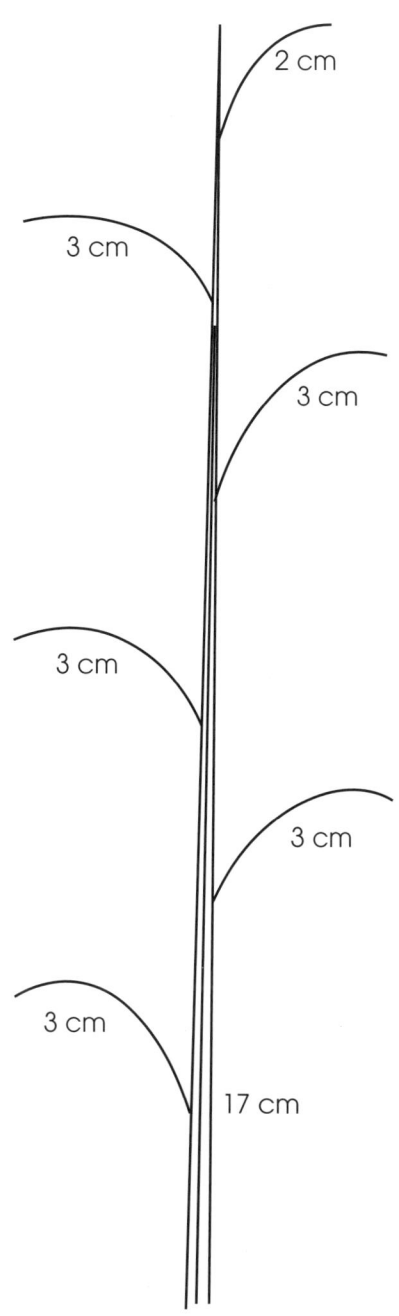

2 cm

3 cm

3 cm

3 cm

3 cm

3 cm

17 cm

Pituri Stem Chart

Buds (Make 4)

For each bud:

Cut 2 white strips 2 mm x 12 cm.

Coil 1 to a short pointed cup. See pattern 74.

Coil 1 to a long rounded end cup. See pattern 75.

Glue open ends together.

74   75

Bud calyx (Make 4)

Cut 1 mid-green strip 1.5 mm x 3 cm, coil to a small tapered cone.

Glue open end over pointed end of bud.

Berries

Cut 2 black strips 2 mm x 12 cm.

Coil 1 to a fat rounded cup. See pattern 76.

Coil 1 to short pointed cup. See pattern 77.

Glue open ends together.

76   77

Main Stem (Make 1)

Make it tapered and laminated and level at one end.

The following are mid-brown:

Cut 1 strip, 3 mm x 17 cm, centre strip.

Cut 2 strips 3 mm x 16 cm, one each side of centre.

Cut 2 strips 3 mm x 15 cm, one each side of 16 cm strips.

Cut 2 strips 3 mm x 12 cm, one each side of 15 cm strips.

Cut 2 strips 3 mm x 10 cm, one each side of 12 cm strips.

Allow to dry completely before mounting.

Secondary Stems

Cut 4 mid-green strips 2 mm x 3 cm, attach on edge.

Cut 1 mid-green strip 2 mm x 2 cm, attach on edge.

Cut 1 mid-brown strip 2 mm x 3 cm, attach on edge towards bottom of main stem.

Leaves

Cut 10 mid-green large leaves from pattern 78.

Cut 9 mid-green small leaves from pattern 79.

Emboss mid rib and curve fine tip around and under the tip of the leaf.

Mounting

Attach stems following the stem chart.

Attach blossoms, then buds.

Attach berries to the one small brown stem near the bottom of the main stem.

Attach larger leaves onto main stem.

Attach smaller leaves onto secondary stems.

Or you can create your own design.

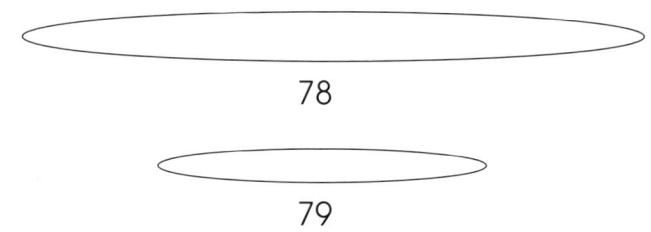

78

79

Pituri — Miniature

(for gift tags 8 cm x 3.5 cm)

Materials

Canson papers
  White (blossoms and bud)
  Yellow (stamen)
  Black (berries)
  Mid-green (calyx, stems and leaves)
Scissors
Fine purple marker or pen
Embossing tool for mid ribs

Construction

Blossoms (Make 4)

For each blossom:
Cut 1 white strip 2 mm x 9 cm.

Stamen

Cut 2 yellow strips 1 mm to a fine point 1 cm long.

Petals

Cut 1 white strip 1 cm x 1.5 cm. Cut from pattern 80.
Press O on the back of each petal and mark the front with purple stripes.
Join pieces as shown in pattern 81.
Coil from stamen end to a tapered cone to 1 cm long.

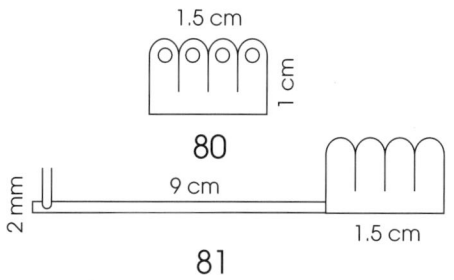

80

81

Calyx

Cut 1 mid-green strip 2 mm x 3 cm and coil to a tapered cone 4 mm long.

Bud

Cut 2 white strips 2 mm x 7 cm.
Coil 1 strip to a stemmed cup.
Coil 1 strip to a rounded cup.
Glue open ends together.

Bud Calyx

Cut 1 mid-green strip 2 mm x 2 cm. Coil to taper 3 mm long.
Glue taper over tip of point of stemmed cup.

Berry

Cut 1 black strip 2 mm x 9 cm. Coil to a rounded cup. Attach to backing by open end.

Stems

Cut from scraps:
2 mid-green strips 1.5 mm x 3 cm.
1 mid-green strip 1.5 mm x 2 cm.

Leaves (cut 3)

Cut leaves in mid-green from pattern 82.
Emboss centre mid rib.

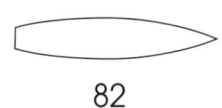

82

Mounting

Mount as pictured or as desired.

LARGE-FLOWERED GUICHENOTIA

Guichenotia macrantha

This delicate looking shrub is really very hardy, being able to survive in the harsh conditions of our deserts. Pale pink to mauve drooping-star flowers appear in winter right through into spring. Being an adaptable plant, it is suitable for home gardens and deserves more attention.

Materials

Canson papers
  Orchid pink (petals)
  Pale green (centres and stigma)
  Mid-brown (stems, leaves and calyx)
  Dark brown (anthers)
Scissors
Embossing tool
Yellow dimensional paint

Construction (needle tool)

Blossoms (Make 12)

For each blossom:

Cut 5-point stars from pattern 83.

Emboss where shown on pattern. Embossed ridges will be on the outside of the star.

Next, using a sharp edge, curl the full length of each star point causing the petal to curl inwards towards the centre.

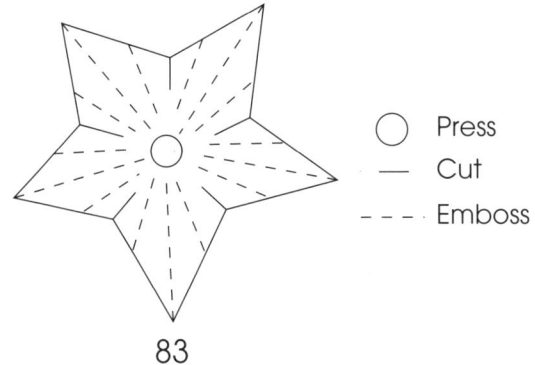

○ Press
— Cut
- - - Emboss

83

Next, make small cuts where shown on pattern and stick overlapping edges. The wider the overlap the tighter the blossom. Vary the overlaps to give an assortment of sizes. See pattern 84.

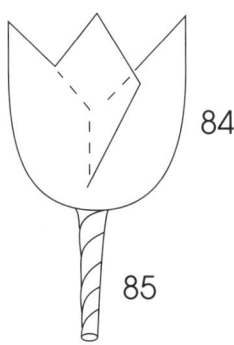

84

85

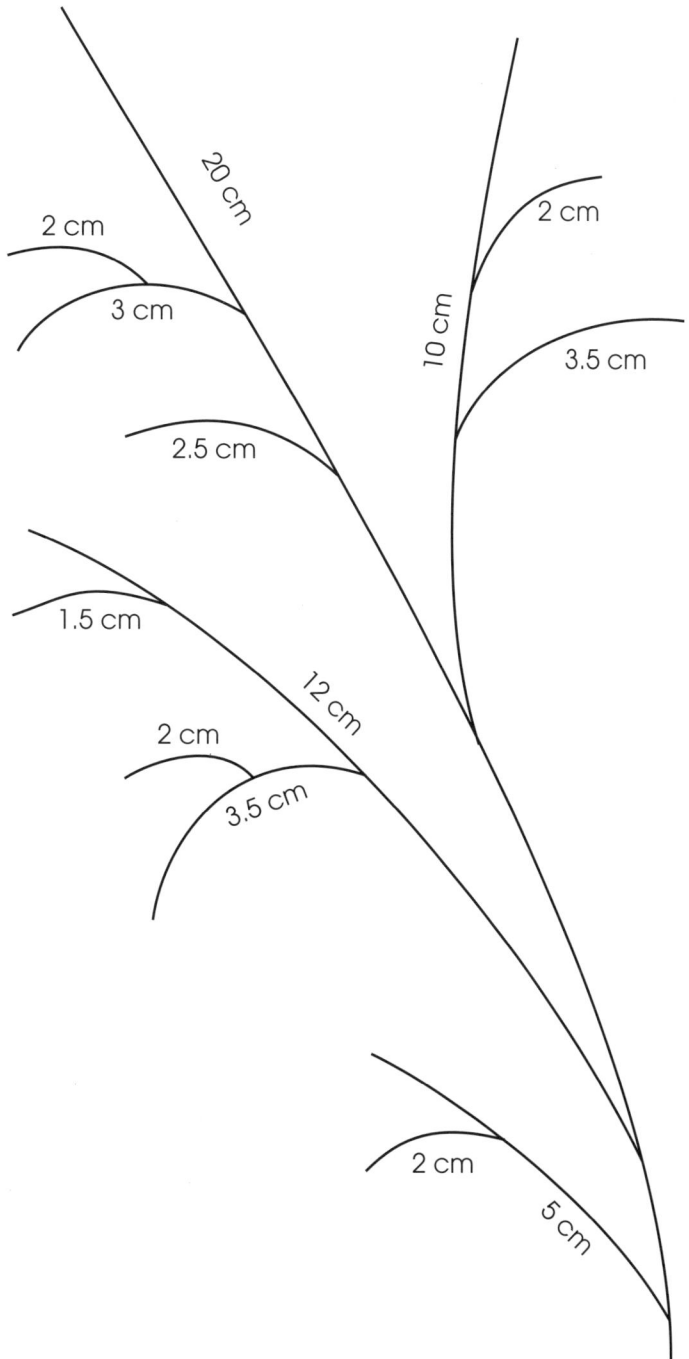

Guichenotia Stem Chart

Calyx

Cut 1 mid-brown strip 4 mm x 6 cm. Coil to a tapered cone 12 mm long.

Attach open end to outside top of the star petals. See pattern 85.

Anthers

(Make 5 for each blossom)

Cut 1 dark brown strip 3 mm x 2 cm. Coil to a tapered cone 5 mm long.

Cut 1 light green strip 1 mm x 7 mm.

Insert and glue one end of the green strip into the widest end of the dark brown cone. Allow at least 5 mm to protrude.

Centre

Cut 1 light green strip 2 mm x 12 cm.

Cut 1 light green strip 1 mm to a fine point 1 cm long for the stigma.

Attach the fine strip to one end of the 12 cm strip at right angles. See pattern 86.

Coil to a domed cup with the fine strip protruding from the top of the dome. See pattern 87.

Tip fine point to stigma with yellow dimensional paint.

When both anthers and centres are dry proceed as follows:

Glue the green stems of the 5 anthers evenly to the sides of the centre. See pattern 88.

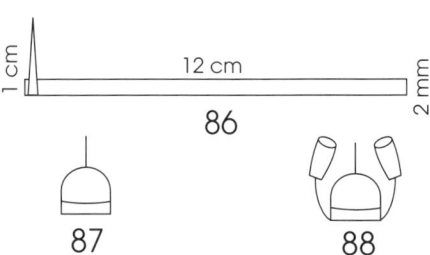

86

87   88

When dry, trim any stem ends that protrude past open end of centre, then glue the open end inside the middle of the star petals.

Leaves

Leaves are attached opposite each other in twos or threes. Place smaller leaves at the tips of stems.

Cut 5 mid-brown small leaves from pattern 89.

Cut 13 mid-brown large leaves from pattern 90.

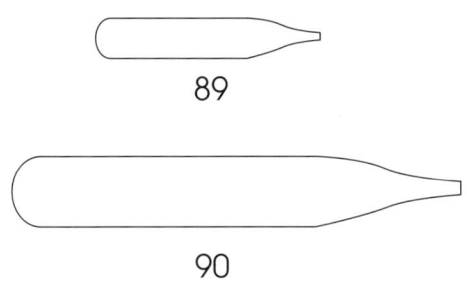

89

90

If you are superstitious cut 14.

Emboss a centre mid rib, fold leaf slightly along this line.

Curl leaf edges back under to give the leaf a rounded edge appearance.

Stems

For main stem (3-layer thickness):

Cut 3 mid-brown strips 2 mm x 20 cm.

For secondary stems (2-layer thickness):

Cut 2 mid-brown strips 2 mm x 12 cm.

Cut 2 mid-brown strips 2 mm x 10 cm.

Cut 2 mid-brown strips 2 mm x 5 cm.

For small mid-brown stems:

Cut 2 strip 2 mm x 3.5 cm.

Cut 1 strips 2 mm x 3 cm.

Cut 1 strip 2 mm x 2.5 cm.

Cut 4 strips 2 mm x 2 cm.

Cut 1 strip 2 mm x 1.5 cm.

Mounting

Position stems as per stem chart.

Position blossoms. Be sure to glue the fine tip

of calyx and also under one star petal too. Position leaves as shown or as you choose.

Guichenotia — Miniature

(for gift tags 8 cm x 3.5 cm)

Materials

Canson papers
    Orchid pink (petals)
    Pale green (centres and calyx)
    Mid brown (leaves)
    Dark brown (anthers)

Construction

Blossoms (Make 5)

Cut 5 pink stars from pattern 91.
Emboss where shown.
Make small cuts where shown.
Curve each petal. It is easier to curve at this point as the small cuts allow for easier curling with better access to each petal.

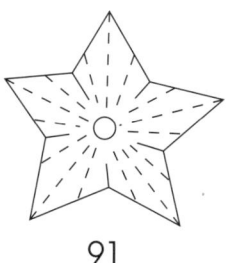

91

Overlap and glue at cuts. The depth of the overlap will depend on your pattern on the cards.

Calyx

Cut 3 pale green strips 2 mm x 3 cm. Taper coil to 7 mm. Attach to blossoms.

Anthers

Cut 1 dark brown strip 1.5 mm x 1 cm.
Cut 1 pale green strip 1.5 mm x 1 cm.
Join at right angles. See pattern 92.
Coil the brown strip around the end of the green strip.

92

Centre

Cut 1 pale green strip 2 mm x 5 cm.
Cut 1 fine pale green tapered strip 1 mm to a fine point x 1 cm long.
Attach following pattern 93.
Tip fine stigma with yellow dimensional paint. Attach anthers evenly around centre.
Coil to a rounded cup. See pattern 94.

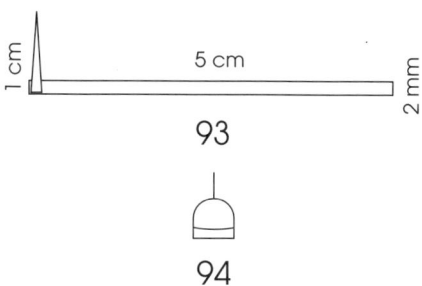

93

94

Leaves

Cut 5 mid-brown leaves from pattern 95 or as many as desired.
Emboss mid rib and curl edges under.

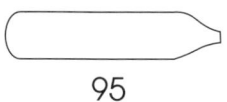

95

Mounting

Mount as pictures or as desired.

POACHED EGG DAISY

Myriocephalus stuartii

This stiff woody herb is an annual resident of the Simpson Desert, where it inhabits the sand dunes. Flowering usually occurs after spring and summer rains have soaked the soil. The common name 'poached egg', as you can see, is quite appropriate. Even though it only grows to 60 cm, it produces a massive amount of seed. Many seeds survive the whole year to start the whole process over again.

Materials

Canson papers
    White (flower edge)
    Yellow (flower centre)
    Pale green (leaves, stems and calyx)
Scissors
Craft knife

Construction (needle tool)

Blossoms (Make 6)
For each blossom:

CENTRE
Cut 1 white strip 3 mm x 17 cm.
Cut 1 yellow strip 1 cm x 27 cm. Fringe only to 3 mm deep. Cut or break the strip into 7 mm sections and tight coil. When the glue is dry, flatten the coil. See patterns 96, 97 and 98. Attach the yellow pieces by the uncut section to the white strip for 15 cm. Evenly space each yellow piece about 1 mm to 2 mm apart. Leave 2 cm of the white strip clear for attachment to white toothed edging strip.

Cut 1 white strip 1 cm x 26 cm. Cut toothed points to within 2 mm of edge. See pattern 99.

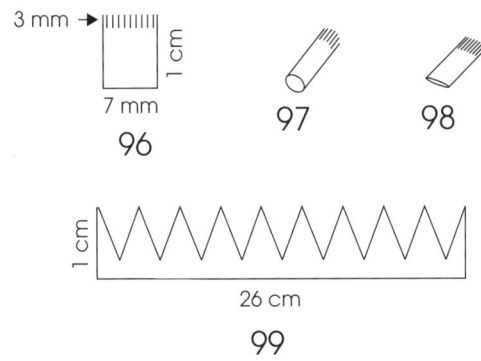

When the 3 mm x 17 cm strip with yellow sections is dry, attach the white toothed strip to the 2 cm clear area. When the glue is dry, coil from the yellow end to a tight coil. When the glue is dry, gently bend the outside row of teeth out and down over the uncut section. Repeat this until all teeth are curved away from the yellow centre. Now spread some of the yellow fringing towards the teeth to close the space between the two colours.

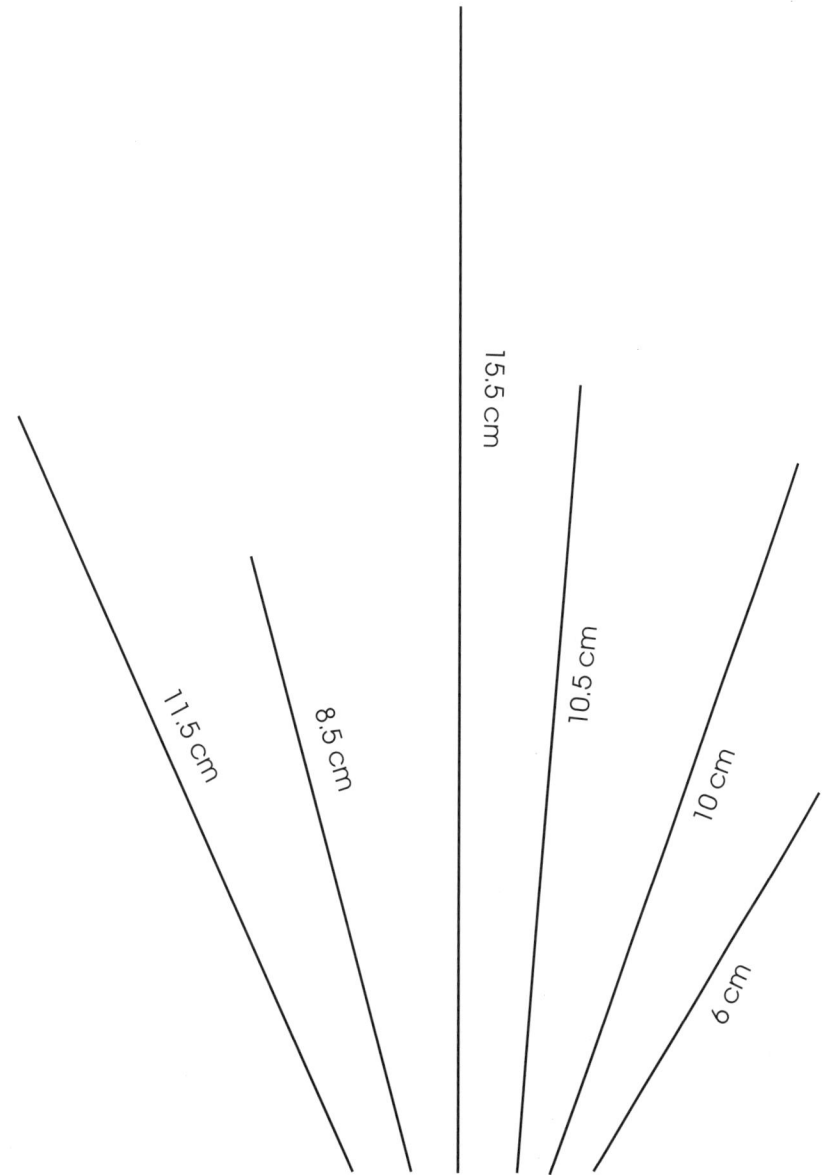

15.5 cm

10.5 cm

11.5 cm

8.5 cm

10 cm

6 cm

Poached Egg Daisy Stem Chart

CALYX (MAKE 4)

Cut 1 pale green strip 2 mm x 87 cm. Tight coil to a stemmed dish shape. See pattern 100. To stabilise the shape, coat the inside with glue and allow to dry before using.

Attach to underside of 4 blossoms.

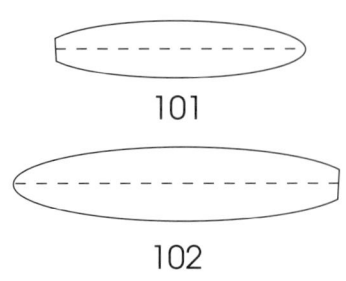

101

102

100

Stems

Cut all strips 1.5cm wide.

Make one of each of these lengths:

15.5 cm

11.5 cm

10.5 cm

10 cm

8.5 cm

6 cm.

Now roll each stem to a tube 3 mm in diameter, overlap edges to join.

Leaves

Cut 6 small pale green leaves from pattern 101.

Cut 22 large pale green leaves from pattern 102.

Emboss mid rib deeply and bend slightly.

Mounting

Following stem chart, attach stem tubes to backing.

Attach leaves alternately down each stem. Place most of smaller leaves on the smaller stems.

Position blossoms to the tip of each tube. Place 2 flat on backing.

For the 4 with calyx, gently curve stalk of the calyx to fit partly down inside open end of stem tube.

Position blossoms at various angles for interest.

Poached Egg Daisy — Miniature

(for gift tags 8 cm x 3.5 cm)

Materials

Canson papers

    White (blossom edge)

    Yellow (blossom centre)

    Pale green (leaves, stems and calyx)

Construction

Blossoms (Make 3)

Cut 1 yellow strip 5 mm x 15 cm, fringe to a depth of 3 mm.

Cut 1 white strip 7 mm x 9 cm. Cut toothed points to within 2 mm of edge. See pattern 103.

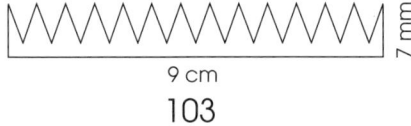

9 cm

7 mm

103

Join strips to one long strip and tight coil from yellow end.

Spread white toothed pieces out and down to cover uncut section then spread some fringing to cover small space between colours.

Calyx (Make 1)

Cut 1 pale green strip 1.5 mm x 18 cm. Coil to a stemmed cup and attach to the base of one blossom.

Leaves

Cut 6 pale green leaves from pattern 104. Emboss mid rib.

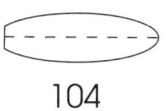

104

Stems

Cut 1 pale green strip 1.5 mm x 6 cm. Fold and glue in three to a 2 cm length.

Construction

Follow the photograph or position as desired.

ROUND-LEAVED PARAKEELYA

Calandrinia remota

T here are a number of parakeelya varieties. Some grow on the sandy coastal strip. Others thrive in the desert sands. The thick fleshy leaves can be used for bush tucker as vegetable greens. The desert varieties often have pinkish red stems and leaves. Flowers appear throughout most of the year, adding a splash of vibrant colour to the landscape.

Materials

Canson papers
>Violet (petals)
>White (centre, stigma and stamen)
>Yellow (stigma cup)
>Pale green (calyx)
>Red earth (stems, leaves and buds)

Gold dimensional paint

Pressing tool for petals

Scissors

Construction (needle tool)

Blossoms (Make 6)

For each blossom:

CENTRES

Cut 1 yellow strip 2 mm x 4 cm.

Cut 1 white strip 2 mm to a fine point 5 mm long for the stigma.

Cut 1 white strip 6 mm x 5 cm, fine fringe to within 1 mm of edge.

Join pieces as shown in pattern 105.

Coil from stigma end, dome yellow section

then straight coil the fringe strip.

Spread fringing out and brush the tips with gold dimensional paint. Allow to dry before adding petals.

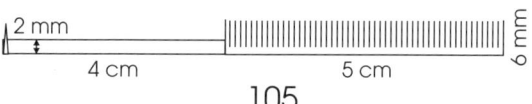

105

PETALS

Cut 5 violet petals from pattern 106.

Using a soft eraser and a round ended tool, press into the petal where shown to create a cup shape.

106

Attach petals by narrow end to uncut section of the centre. Overlap the widest part of the petals in the same direction. The petals' narrow ends should fit neatly around the centre.

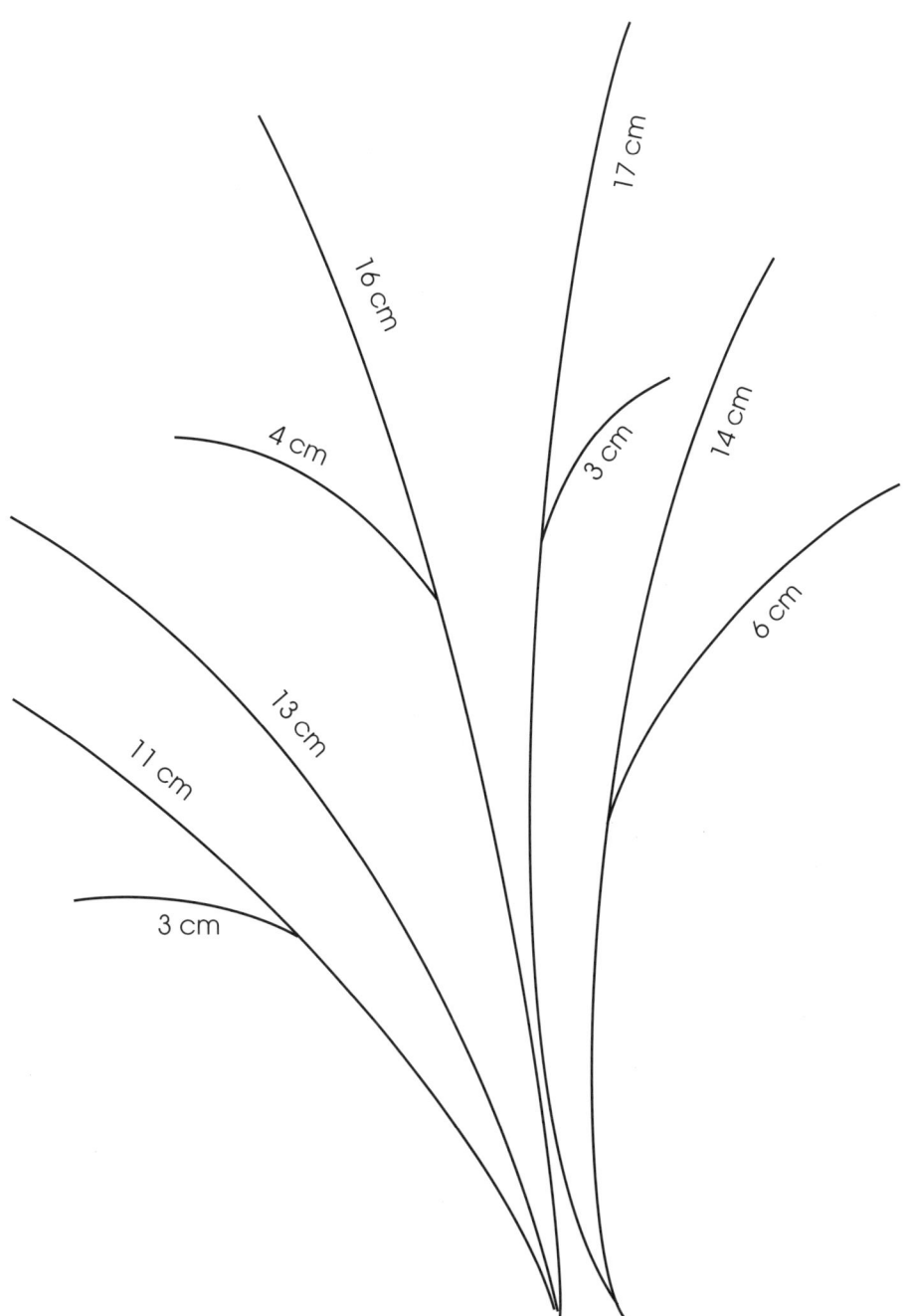

Parakeelya Stem Chart

CALYX — FOR BLOSSOM (MAKE 2)

Cut 1 light green strip 2 mm x 12 cm. Coil to a stemmed cup following pattern 107. Attach to base of blossoms.

107

Buds (Make 3)

Cut 1 red earth strip 2 mm x 10 cm. Coil long cone 1 cm long. See pattern 108.

108

CALYX — FOR BUD

Cut 1 light green strip 2 mm x 9 cm. Coil to a stemmed cup. See pattern 109.
Glue calyx to open end of bud.

109

Leaves

These are quilled with a needle tool. Glue as you go if needed.
Make 4 large leaves. For each:
Cut 1 red earth strip 5 mm x 70 cm. Coil carefully to a long tapered cone 5 cm long.
Make 1 small leaf.

Cut 1 red earth strip 3 mm x 52 cm. Coil carefully to a long tapered cone 3 cm long.
Coat the inside of cones with glue for stability. Allow to dry thoroughly.
Shape open end as shown to reduce the size of opening for attachment to base of plant. See patterns 110, 111 and 112.
Flatten leaves lengthways but allow them to spring back slightly.

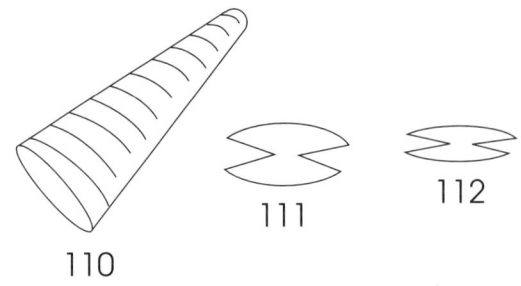

110   111   112

Stems (3-layer thickness)

Cut 3 red earth strips 3 mm x 17 cm.
Cut 3 red earth strips 3 mm x 16 cm.
Cut 3 red earth strips 3 mm x 14 cm.
Cut 3 red earth strips 3 mm x 13 cm.
Cut 3 red earth strips 3 mm x 11 cm.
Cut 3 red earth strips 3 mm x 6 cm.
Cut 3 red earth strips 3 mm x 4 cm.
Cut 3 red earth strips 3 mm x 3 cm.

Mounting

Position stems following the stem chart.
Next add blossoms and buds.
Cluster leaves around base of stems.
Add leaves by glued open end. Do not glue entire leaf down onto backing. Support each leaf at an angle while it dries.

Parakeelya — Miniature

(for gift tags 8 cm x 3.5 cm)

Materials

Canson papers

    Violet (petals)

    White (centre, stigma and stamen)

    Yellow (stigma cup)

    Pale green (calyx)

    Red earth (stems, leaves and buds)

Gold dimensional paint

Pressing tool and soft eraser

Construction

Blossoms (Make 3)

For each blossom:

CENTRE

Cut 1 yellow strip 1.5 mm x 2 cm.

Cut 1 white strip 1 mm tapered to a fine point x 5 mm long for the stigma.

Cut 1 white strip 5 mm x 2.5 cm. Fine fringe to within 1 mm of the edge.

Join strips as shown in pattern 113.

Coil as shown in pattern 114.

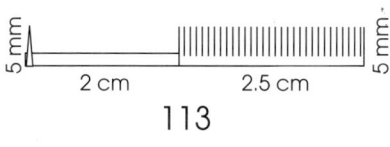

113

114

Dome yellow strip then straight coil fringing strip.

Brush fringing tips with gold dimensional paint.

PETALS

Cut 5 violet petals as shown in pattern 115. Press centre of petal to cup shape.

115

Attach stems of petal to uncut section of centre fringing.

CALYX (MAKE 1)

Cut 1 pale green strip 1.5 mm x 7 cm. Tight coil to stemmed cup.

Attach to base of blossom.

Buds (Make 2)

Cut 1 red earth strip 2 mm x 5 cm. Coil a long taper 6 mm long.

BUD CALYX (MAKE 2)

Cut 1 pale green strip 1.5 mm x 5 cm. Coil to stemmed cup.

Attach to open end of buds.

Leaf (Make 1)

Cut 1 red earth strip 2 mm x 18 cm. Coil a long cone 1.5 cm long. Coat inside with glue. for strength. See pattern 116.

116

Mounting

Mount as shown or as desired.

When dry press open end closed.

Stems

Cut 1 red earth strip 2 mm x 3 cm. Attach on edge.

Cut 1 red earth strip 2 mm x 2.5 cm. Attach on edge.

Cut 1 red earth strip 2 mm x 1 cm. Attach on edge.